ELIJAH'S
MANTLE

OTHER PARKER BOOKS

African American Church Leadership, edited by Lee N. June
  and Christopher C. Mathis Jr
Making Your Vision a Reality by Paul Cannings

PARKER BOOKS

ELIJAH'S
MANTLE

Empowering
the Next Generation
of African American
Christian Leaders

Diane Proctor Reeder
Editor

Kregel
Ministry

Elijah's Mantle: Empowering the Next Generation of African American Christian Leaders

© 2013 by Diane Proctor Reeder

Published by Kregel Publications, a division of Kregel, Inc., P.O. Box 2607, Grand Rapids, MI 49501.

Parker Books was conceived by Matthew Parker, the president of the Institute for Black Family Development, Detroit, MI, and is an imprint that provides books for Christian ministry leaders.

All Scripture quotations, unless otherwise indicated, are from the Holy Bible, New International Version®, NIV®. Copyright© 1973, 1978, 1984, 2011 by Biblica, Inc.™ Used by permission of Zondervan. All rights reserved worldwide. www.zondervan.com

Scripture quotations marked NLT are from the Holy Bible, New Living Translation, copyright © 1996, 2004, 2007 by Tyndale House Foundation. Used by permission of Tyndale House Publishers, Inc., Carol Stream, Illinois 60188. All rights reserved.

Scripture quotations marked NKJV are from the New King James Version®. Copyright © 1982 by Thomas Nelson, Inc. Used by permission. All rights reserved.

Scripture quotations marked NASB are from the New American Standard Bible®. Copyright © 1960, 1962, 1963, 1968, 1971, 1972, 1973, 1975, 1977, 1995 by The Lockman Foundation. Used by permission. www.Lockman.org

Scripture quotations marked KJV are from the King James Version.

ISBN 978-0-8254-4303-9

Printed in the United States of America
13 14 15 16 17 / 5 4 3 2 1

To all our Elijahs, from all our Elishas

CONTENTS

CONTRIBUTORS

Matt Parker, president of The Parker Organization LLC

Dolphus Weary, president of The Real Christian Foundation

Paul Cannings, pastor of Living Word Fellowship Church of Houston and president of Power Walk Ministry

Sabrina Black, cofounder of Girls with Great Potential

Michael and Maria Westbrook, copastors, Greater Life, Inc.

Russell Knight, founding president, Chicago Urban Reconciliation Enterprise, Inc.

Roland G. Hardy Jr., president of Roland Hardy & Associates

Diane Proctor Reeder, president of Written Images

BRICKS WITHOUT STRAW

There is a popular line in the African American community. It is a storyline rooted in the oral history of America, a line deeply etched into the fabric of American society. For African Americans, it is a toxic storyline that lays blame. It is a harsh judge, a stealer of hope, a killer of dreams.

The line goes something like this: "When are Black people ever going to get it together? Other ethnic groups find ways to work together; why are we always acting like crabs in a barrel? Slavery was over a long time ago; we have to stop acting like victims."

We take issue with that line of thinking. First of all, the last enslaved African American, Charlie Smith, only died in 1979. The last child of an enslaved African American died in the twenty-first century. So we see that slavery is not the ancient history that some make it out to be. But secondly, and more importantly, there are a number of contingents of African Americans who are defying, challenging, and daring the stereotypes.

These individuals are all around us. Their untold stories abound, and have the potential to empower generations of African Americans.

In 1984, I gathered a group of African American evangelical leaders from around the nation to participate in a historic gathering that allowed us to share some of those stories and strategies, but most importantly to interact with an eye towards learning, collaboration, and growth. We refined that group, and now one hundred leaders who comprise "The Summit" meet annually.

I was in conversation with members of the African Christian Fellowship when a question came up. "We have to discuss why Africans who come to this country are more successful than African Americans who are already here," said a member of the organization.

11

That's not true for everyone. The children of our Summit members are doing quite well. They are college graduates, doctors, teachers, ministers, and business owners. They are, in their own way, working the way we have tried to work to "turn the world upside down."

It is true that African Americans lag behind their white counterparts on a number of measures, when taken as a whole. In *Succession of Leadership*, we lay out that historical narrative in a way that aids in understanding the development of Black America. Part One, "Living Epistles," lays out the "present state" of a select group of members of the Summit, a organization of Christian leaders that encourages members to network and help each other reach their God-given visions. Finally, Part Two, "Living Principles," Summit members lay out a roadmap of principles, tactics, and strategies for effective ministry leadership.

In every successful people group, there is an intergenerational passing of information, resources, and contacts. When that happens for several hundred years—as is the case with those people groups who were not subjected to the stripping of language, customs, and culture—the group can grow in strength upon a firm foundation.

Unfortunately, that did not happen with African Americans, as the poem[1] below illustrates:

Bricks Without Straw

Bricks without straw
Bricks without straw
is how we came over

a piece of memory here
(most of it obliterated when they banned our native tongues)

a Bible verse there
(concocted to mold obedience
but we looked deeper, further
into its real truth…and created a whole 'nother kind of church…)

---

1. The poem "Bricks Without Straw," © 2004 Diane Proctor Reeder. Used by permission.

Introduction

Bricks without straw
Bricks without straw
is how we came over

Everybody else brought their culture over intact
the family ties, the rituals
the businesses and institutions
the language
whole cloth   no worms that ate holes through them
        no evil and gnarled hands to rend the cloth
into shreds

Make bricks without straw
they shouted to us
holding the straw in their hands
controlling even the bricks of our existence

What's wrong with you   Can't you get yourself together

And now we ask ourselves   the same thing

We forget.

Bricks without straw
Bricks without straw
is how we came over

So we took what little we were given
a piece of cloth, a pig's intestine, a plot of land,
        a word, a verse, a memory

a corpse

and waved our spirit-wand over the whole lot,
pieces and things and children and spouses and brothers and sisters
        and cousins and friends

And up jumped whole cloth, buildings
wrestled up from nothing but dirt
schools and funeral societies and banks and insurance companies
    and picket fence homes and whole new church denominations
    where none had been
and deacons and ushers and choirs and songs to remember our story . . .

A story made from bricks
without straw
but with much blood   prayer   tears   sweat
and groanings that cannot be uttered.

The Summit's strategy is not to bemoan the condition of African Americans. Rather, it is to build on a legacy of African American Christian leadership, paying special attention to its history of strength, integrity, intellect, and honor in the face of impossible circumstances.

The stories of successful African American evangelical ministries abound. These stories are all but hidden from the mainstream media, which seems to revel in painting a different picture—a picture of lack and dysfunction. But before we draw our conclusions, let's take a step back. This first chapter, "The Narrative," will help us do that.

PART ONE: LIVING EPISTLES

Examples of Effective Leadership Succession

Ye are our epistle
written in our hearts,
known and read of all men.
~2 Cor. 3:2 KJV

Chapter 1

THE NARRATIVE: HOW WE GOT HERE

Matt Parker

The sweeping history of African American development finds its genesis in Africa and then moves across the Atlantic to the Americas, where twists and turns of circumstances and God's providence combine to create a scenario that includes the entire sweep of the human drama, from the tragedy of broken families to the quiet success of the extended family that served Black families so well—a concept deeply, almost genetically, rooted in the African village model of community.[1]

In August of 1619, Antony and Isabella Pedro, and other Africans, stepped ashore to what is now the state of Virginia. Thus began the history of Africans in America. Antony and Isabella were married, and around 1623 gave birth to the first African American child. They named him William, and baptized him under the auspices of the Church of England.

They came, these first African Americans, as indentured servants and enjoyed the same status of White indentured servants who sold their services for a stipulated number of years. The available evidence suggests that most of this first generation of African Americans worked out their terms of servitude and were freed.

But the history of African Americans reaches back much further, into

---

1. This chapter has been adapted from Matt Parker, *Teaching Our Men, Reaching Our Fathers* (Detroit: Parker Books, 2010)

the distant past when the great African Sudanese empires of Ghana, Akrum, Mali, Songhai, Meroe, Egypt, and Ethiopia flourished on the African continent. Lerone Bennett Jr., in his book *Before the Mayflower,* says:

"It is already reasonable, in fact, to believe that the African ancestors of African Americans were among the major benefactors of the human race. Blacks, or people who would be considered Blacks today, were among the first people to use tools, paint pictures, plant seeds, and worship gods. They founded empires and states. They made some of the critical discoveries and contributions that led to the modern world."

Despite stellar achievements in these and many other areas, the image of African Americans is negative and no one seems immune to that characterization. African American men are automatically suspect. They are often judged without a trial or jury—even before all the facts come to light.

There is very little awareness of the contributions that African Americans have made to science, medicine, history, and civilization. The National Task Force on African American Men and Boys, chaired by activist and former United Nations ambassador Andrew Young, published "Repairing the Breach," which identifies a number of African American males who have succeeded at all levels of American society. The report points to Dr. Benjamin Carson, a world authority on brain surgery and the first neurosurgeon to successfully separate Siamese twins joined at the head. It mentions Colin Powell, the first African American ever to head the post of chairman of the Joint Chiefs of Staff and later served as President George W. Bush's secretary of state. It heralds Garrett Morgan's invention of the traffic light, making urban travel safe for all. It was released a few years before the historic election of Barack Obama as the first African American president of the United States.

Not only that. As we celebrate the election of our first African American president, Barack Obama, we must also remember the late Shirley Chisholm, the first African American—man or woman—to run for president under the Democratic Party. Her courage paved the way.

There is the late U.S. Congresswoman Barbara Jordan, who spoke so eloquently about integrity during impeachment proceedings against President Richard Nixon; or the first African American female secretary of state, Condoleezza Rice. Not to mention the named and unnamed church mothers who teach young women, chastise the boys to mind their manners, and command respect from everyone because of their own above-reproach reputations.

One common thread unites our many past and present Black heroes: They all had to overcome tremendous obstacles and take on singularly difficult challenges. We must continue to remind America, African American people in particular, and the world that one of the great characteristics of African Americans is the ability to overcome all challenges—past, present, and future.

At one time, the African American church was a strong, pervasive, and revered institution. Young people who had no problem stealing, cheating, and purse snatching wouldn't dare pursue their illegal activities in the proximity of a church. While they might curse and fight in school, they would be careful to be polite to the preachers, the deacons, and the "mothers" in the church.

All that has changed drastically. There are reasons for this, and there are ways to address the problem. African American churches of today have a great opportunity for leadership in the spiritual, social, political, and economic development of African Americans.

The African American church movement started in the late 1770s with the founding of the first churches in South Carolina, Virginia, Philadelphia, Georgia, and New York. Churches were founded by free men and women as well as those who remained enslaved. The church was the place where leadership was taught and where people benefited from economic, political, and social education in addition to being taught the Word of God. God's Word was made relevant to the African American condition at the time. Most of our historical leaders came from the African American church. Throughout history, these churches provided social, political, economic, and spiritual leadership for many in the African American community.

It was a necessary development. After all, the Christian church established during the two hundred-plus years of African enslavement in this country was an overtly all-White, or all-European, institution with little or no room for persons of color. African Americans were not welcome. In fact, it may surprise some to learn that the legal prohibition against Blacks and Whites marrying was overturned only well into the civil rights movement, in 1967 by the U.S. Supreme Court in the *Loving v. Virginia* decision. At the time, sixteen states still had that marriage prohibition on their books.

In fact, evangelical churches on the whole were diametrically opposed to any efforts to address the issue of racial equality from its first stirrings during the U.S.-sanctioned enslavement of Blacks to the civil rights movement that began in the 1950s. It has been established that members of many

White evangelical churches were actually also Ku Klux Klan members, and that pastors held the status quo of overt and covert racism even when the very concept became less and less popular as national policy.

Without the intervention of the church to mount a strong faith-based response to the sin of racism, racism was free to do its damage. And damage it did, with an overrepresentation of drugs in African American communities, an overrepresentation of poor educational conditions, and an underrepresentation of financial investment in increasingly Black cities.

The Black church held firm, working against the odds to anchor communities and remain relevant. Unfortunately, the damage had been done and the economic and social devastation contributed to a decline in family stability and a rise in drug use, health disparities, and poverty. But numbers don't tell the whole story. The real story is that African Americans continued to strive and excel, even in the most dire of circumstances. Instead of focusing on the reasons for our failure, why not focus on the factors in our success, and then build on that?

Statistics can distort. Many of you have heard it repeated that "There are more African American men in prison than in college." Now it is true that African American men are overrepresented in the criminal justice system, and that is a reality that must be addressed. But the statistical data simply no longer bears out that statement. In 2009, 919,000 Black men were enrolled in college, and 827,000 Black men were in prison. Add to the fact that we are comparing apples and oranges, because most college students are in their twenties. If we were to do a more realistic comparison, we would compare the number of Black men in their twenties in college to the number of Black men in their twenties in prison—which would make the gap even wider. And how many of you knew that the number of Black men in prison is actually on the decline, as is the number of unwed pregnancies in the African American community? We and the mainstream are so much quicker to trumpet our bad news than our good news.

The twenty-first century has ushered in a revival in many of our African American churches. These churches believe that they can achieve something that no other institution or program has yet been able to do: create a nurturing, learning, healing place for African American men, women and families. In so doing, churches can provide the self-respect, confidence, and spiritual grounding that we must have to build our communities and our world.

Chapter 2

THE SUMMIT GROUP:
IMPACTING THE WORLD

Matt Parker

T he Summit Group is a mustard seed group of African American Christian leadership that is slowly transforming the way mission and ministry is done in the African American community... and paving the way towards cross-cultural, national, and international ministry partnerships.

To explain the development of The Summit, I first must tell you about myself. Born in 1945, I was mentored by my parents, Matt and Ruth Parker, wise woman Barbara Walton, Lloyd Blue, and evangelist Tom Skinner. They have all since made their transition.

My educational development began in the Detroit Public School system. A brief stint at a Grand Rapids, Michigan junior college followed; but my pivotal moment came at Grand Rapids School of Bible and Music, where I committed my life to Christ. It was there where I also "discovered" an untold story of racism within the white Christian church, a revelation that informs my life's work even today. I ended up working with a number of Eurocentric Christian institutions, including Campus Crusade for Christ; Athletes in Action, a Christian sports ministry; Wheaton College in Illinois; and William Tyndale College, where I developed a celebrated urban studies program that resulted in a number of graduates developing ministry organizations and projects in cities around the country.

Chapter 2

From 1984–2008, I gathered Christian leaders every two years to network and share resources with each other. This "National Summit on Black Church Development" emphasized the importance of the Black Church to the community, but also the importance of collaborating along racial lines on a peer basis with white Christian evangelicals. That is extremely important: Christian institutions of color have for too long had a dominant-submissive relationship with white Christian institutions, and God never designed for one culture to dominate the other; rather, relationships were intended to develop on a level plane, based upon oneness in the body of Christ, and upon equality of importance to the body.

> **There is neither Jew nor Gentile**, *neither slave nor free, nor is there male and female, for you are all **one** in Christ Jesus.*
> ~Gal. 3:28

> *But God has put the body together, giving greater honor to the parts that lacked it, so that there should be no division in the body, but that its parts should have equal concern for each other.*
> ~1 Cor. 12:24–25

These Summit meetings, which now happen annually, have proven fruitful. I have deliberately and intentionally encouraged Summit attendees to network and collaborate on projects independent of The Summit's activities, and they have. The results speak for themselves:

- Thirty-five churches, organizations, projects have been launched.

- Summit members and their organizations have received $50 million in book sales, products, training, and in-kind contributions.

- Six hundred leaders received one thousand hours of networking, coaching, and equipping.

The Billy Graham Center Archives on Evangelism and Missions now serves as the repository for the oral and written records of twenty Summit leaders; the Destiny '87 Congress on Missions; and the Atlanta '88 Congress on Evangelizing Black America.

Matt Parker

On June 24, 2010, we established The Summit Group to equip one hundred African American leaders to reproduce other leaders around the world. We had already started this work, and the formal establishment of The Summit Group was a culmination and recognition of the work we have accomplished to date. This group now serves more than one million people internationally.

We believe in "seeding" efforts nationally and internationally. The Summit Group has established a role for itself of "planting" visions, perspective, and ideas, and then bringing ministry leaders together to collaborate on the work necessary for those ideas to grow and develop. We add in the important component of training and information to help leaders raise money and plan/manage effectively. We then allow those projects to take on a life of their own, which allows for the freedom necessary to expand in God's timing and according to his plans.

The mission of The Summit is to identify, develop, and empower African American leaders to equip other world leaders to serve children, youth, and families by providing training, networking, technical assistance and resource materials. Its goal is to increase the capacity to reproduce other world leaders to collaborate in evangelizing and making disciples in the world according to Matthew 28:16–20, Acts 13:1, and Acts 17:26. This is a sacred calling, and the Summit exists to come alongside leaders and support that calling.

With calling in place, the Summit has now forged a number of partnerships and initiatives designed to develop leaders. First, The Summit established a joint venture, under its affiliate Parker Books, with Kregel Publications to publish titles on leadership authored by Summit members. A second joint venture with Radio Bible Class Ministries, "Summit Group University," will offer free and fee-based courses on leadership at www.summitgroup.christiancourses.com. A third joint venture is with Willow Creek's Global Leadership Summit in Illinois, a dynamic annual two-day event that is seen in more than 450 locations and more than seventy countries around the globe—upward of 185,000 people. The plan is to engage Willow Creek in a partnership to ensure that African American leadership is represented in the annual participation as well as planning of the event. Finally, we established an organization, Detroit Partnership—a city-suburban network of churches that is focused on wholistic ministry collaborations in a context of genuine racial reconciliation.

Chapter 2

HOW DID WE DO IT?

On February 5, 2006, 2,100 volunteers from across Metropolitan Detroit served nearly 9,000 Detroiters with food, social services, and hope. The volunteers came from more than forty churches and nearly every denomination. They came from the city proper and from distant suburbs. They were Black, White, and Hispanic. They were in one spot on one day with one purpose: to reach the people God loves with the gospel, with prayer, and with sustenance to help them live better, fuller lives.

That day did not happen in a vacuum. It was the culmination of a decades-long story of ministry launchings, educational experiences, and lessons learned; a result of much prayer, conflict, and resolution. It is an ongoing story of reconciliation: reconciliation of man with God, and of man with man.

We began with a Summit on Black Church Development in 1984. More than fifty African American church leaders came together to talk about ways to ensure that the Black Church become more responsive to the spiritual and physical needs of the communities in which they live and serve. We ended up with a cogent, powerful document that served as a basis for our work going forward.

At the same time, I was working closely with White Christian leadership, challenging those institutions to carefully consider the charge of racism and to address those charges with frank, peer-to-peer conversations with Black Christian leaders about a shared response that would be consistent with the truest elements of the gospel of Jesus Christ.

As a result, we saw The Summit morph into an annual interracial, intergenerational, interdenominational meeting of Black and White Christians with the goal of engaging in relationships guided by the biblical principles of partnership, mentorship, networking, documentation, and sharing.

PARTNERSHIPS

We learned some very important lessons in this nearly thirty-year journey. The first thing we learned:

Effective partnerships are built on trusting relationships and led by the Holy Spirit.

The heart of the gospel is restored relationships. In addressing relationships,

Matt Parker

we demonstrate the outworking of the essence and evidence of salvation. Leadership (facilitators, steering committees, etc.) must be very intentional about building this quality of relationships.

Effective partnerships need a facilitator.

The facilitator must have a burning commitment to both the vision and outcomes as well as to partnership as a means of realizing the vision. This person is committed to both the individual ministries and their common success. He/she is both prophet and servant and must be specifically selected, trained, coached, and encouraged in this critical role of a facilitator.

> *"So we decided, having come to complete agreement, to send you official representatives..."*
>
> ~Acts 15:25 NLT

Effective partnerships are about a compelling, commonly acknowledged/held vision.

The vision must be articulated in outcomes that are specific and objectively measurable. Good fellowship is not enough. Articulating the vision and the measurable outcomes provide the basis for strategy and tactics as well as a sense of accomplishment. Structure should never be greater than absolutely necessary.

> *"It seemed good to the Holy Spirit and to us not to burden you with anything beyond the following requirements..."*
>
> ~Acts 15:28

Effective partnerships have limited, achievable objectives.

Setting objectives with high priority as well as reasonable potential for success is critical in the early stages. Objectives with results that cannot possibly be seen for years cause discouragement and lead to partnership breakdowns, as participants work hard but do not see any evidence that their work is making an impact.

Effective partnerships are a process, not an event.

It's just like building a building. In a large, multi-level building, much preparation is necessary. First, the designer/architect must articulate what the building should look like on the outside. Then, the inside must be planned. How many rooms? What will be the purpose/function of each room? How large will they be? Then there are the blueprints. The engineers have to test whether the vision for the building is feasible from an engineering standpoint. They have to make sure that the building materials will be adequate to hold up the structure and accommodate the function. This is a protracted process and while it is going on, those waiting for the building to be completed will not see much evidence of progress.

The effective partnership will be the same way. The prospective partners will have to do significant planning to ensure that the partnership works, that everyone is on the same page, and that goals and methods are clearly communicated.

Effective partnerships are made up of partners with clear identities and vision.

The clearer a partner's vision and identity, the more assured they will be in their potential role and their ability to effectively contribute. Each partner must see the value of the partnership to their vision and feel as though their contribution is important and valued by the other partners.

Effective partnerships focus on what they have in common.

Vision and purpose draw ministries together. Having a well-defined "end" is critical. A focus on the "means"—particularly at the early stages—can lead to division.

Effective partnerships acknowledge and meet expectations of key constituencies.

All effective partnerships have at least four constituencies: the audience or group they are seeking to serve or reach, the active partners, the leadership of each partner ministry, and those funding and praying for each partner ministry. Each of these constituencies will have a particular set of priorities and needs. Partners need to be able to effectively communicate the outcomes of the partnership in terms their constituency understands and values.

ETHNIC PARTNERSHIPS

Ethnic issues have plagued the church since the first century. The book of Acts chronicles one such issue. The Jews, biblically identified as the "chosen people" of God, were a distinct ethnic group with religious as well as cultural traditions. A dispute arose when the church's leaders were led by the Holy Spirit to accept Gentiles into the Christian faith. The argument was over whether those Gentiles would be required to adhere to all of the Old Testament laws and Jewish customs as part of their faith commitment. As a compromise, the leaders agreed that Gentile males would not have to be circumcised to be accepted as Christians, but would instead simply have to agree to a subset of laws relative to diet, premarital sexual relations, and idol worship.

The same is true today.

Manifest Destiny is the belief in the 1840s in the inevitable territorial expansion of the United States—the eastern colonies' superior belief that God gave the right to civilize land, people, and culture all the way to the west. Gradually, by force, eastern colonies extended their control throughout North America, regarding Indians and Mexicans as little more than a nuisance to be pushed out of the way. These beliefs have caused the bloodiest wars of conquest and the destruction of peoples who stood in the paths of spreading civilization.

In 1884 at the Berlin Conference, Africa, as the second largest continent in the world, was partitioned among the British, French, Belgian, Portuguese, and other European powers. The reasoning was that possession of precious metals, gems, raw materials, land, cheap labor, and other resources should not be in the ownership of uncivilized people.

This belief that comes out of European doctrine has impacted the world. Today in the United States it is called "White Privilege."

It is said that Sunday morning 11 a.m. is the most segregated hour of the week. We speak of the "Black Church" as a separate entity, and that is because the "White Church" initially did not welcome African Americans into the inner sanctum of the faith. This superior attitude cannot be successful in working with many ethnic people in neighborhoods and cities.

And so, we come to our first principle of effective **ethnic** partnerships:

Effective ethnic partnerships openly acknowledge differ-ences in histories and traditions ... even to the point of celebrating these differences.

This acknowledges that "ears" are not" eyes," and that Jews, Greeks, Romans, and Samaritans with their enormous cultural/traditional differ-ences were all welcome in the kingdom vision. Paul spells it out beautifully in the book of Galatians: "There is neither Jew nor Gentile, neither slave nor free, nor is there male and female, for you are all one in Christ Jesus" (Gal. 3:28).

An ethnic partnership is one that is compassionate and sensitive to all ethnic groups. While respecting the ethnic group uniqueness, an ethnic partnership takes into account the needs of the people, and structures a positive program response to meet it.

An effective ethnic partnership is characterized by multi-cultural leadership.

Historically, when Blacks and Whites agreed to work together in ministry, the White Christians tended to assume the mantle of leadership. That does not work in the twenty-first century, when hard-fought rights have been won and old prejudices have been exposed as not only outmoded, but morally of-fensive as well. Stories of sad ministry collapses abound that are character-ized by the failure to accept minority leadership.

The Antioch church described in Acts 13 is a perfect example of this. This church was led by a genuinely multicultural team that included Barnabas, a Levite; Simon Niger, whose name and title indicates that he was a dark-skinned African; Lucius Cyrene, a North African; Manaen, a Palestinian; and Paul, a Hebraic Jew. It was here that followers of Jesus Christ were first called "Christians."

And that leadership must include ownership also. Otherwise, the relation-ship becomes subservient in nature, where one group can exercise control over another based upon that group holding financial sway. There must be a col-laboration on financial policies and arrangements that is mutually agreed upon, not dictated from the side of the partnership that possesses the most resources.

Self-esteem must be a core value in ethnic partnerships.

In this partnership, we must agree that individuals must have a good opinion of their own dignity and worth. This is vital to any successful initiative. See these other verses for a full perspective on ethnic ministry:

- Genesis 1:27
- Genesis 9:25–27
- Genesis 10:9–32
- Jonah 1–4
- Zephaniah 1–4
- Matthew 8:5–13
- Matthew 28:16–20
- John 1:44–46
- John 4:1–42
- Acts 1:8
- Acts 17:26
- Acts 17:26–28
- Galatians 3:26–28
- Ephesians 2:13–16
- Philemon 1:1–25
- James 2:1–26

MENTORSHIP

Mentorship—that is, strengthening, encouraging and protecting men and women in ministry—is one of the most fundamental and significant ways we can influence history. You will never know what the person you mentor may accomplish, never know how many people they will reach, or never know what important movements might be started. Mentorship has been key to the success of the Detroit Partnership and other ministries developed out of that first 1984 Summit.

Mentoring is a lifelong relationship in which a mentor helps a protégé reach his or her God-given potential. It touches every area of life:

- family and marriage
- financial

- personal growth
- physical
- professional
- social
- spiritual

Mentoring is a *multiplication process*. Barnabas mentored Paul and Timothy mentored Titus. They spent time together, and the protégés "caught" the way the mentor lived, taught, interacted with others, and responded to challenges. It is a pathway, a bridge, and a process that allows many protégés to grow into mature adulthood. It leads to increased success, transformation in values, and sometimes to lifelong business or ministry relationships.

Mentors should be careful to be honest and transparent with their protégés. They should not only be teachers, but deeply committed to seeing that their protégés become exactly who God intended them to be. If you are a protégé, your mentor should believe in your potential, help you define your dream, and be proficient at helping you develop the plan to execute your dream in a godly way. He or she should be open to learning from you as well as teaching you, and avoid prioritizing his or her own agenda above yours. Conversely, you as a protégé should be teachable, faithful, accountable, transparent, and a good steward of your God-given gifts as well as the material gifts of others.

NETWORKING

Networking is a decentralized, non-hierarchical process. It is people talking to each other, sharing ideas, information, and resources. It is a verb, not a noun. The importance is the process, not the product. It is the information communication that creates linkages between people and groups.

Networking is done by conferences, phone calls, air travel, books, organizations, papers, pamphleteering, photocopying, lectures, workshops, parties, grapevines, mutual friends, summit meetings, coalitions, tapes, and newsletters. Networks exist to foster self-help, to exchange information, to change society, to improve productivity and work life, and to share resources. They are structured to transmit information in a way that is quicker, more high-touch, and more energy-efficient that any other process we know.

Matt Parker

Structurally, the most important thing about networking is that each individual is at its center. Within the networking structure, information itself is the great equalizer. Networking functions as a human clearinghouse for ideas. Networking empowers people to nurture one another.

In all of our activities, from the Institute on Black Family Development to The Summit to Detroit Partnership, we emphasized the importance of networking—and most importantly, provided ample opportunities for our partners to do just that. Every year at The Summit, we literally schedule a block of time for people interested in a given ministry area to gather in a room and ... talk. The ministries and shared initiatives that have come out of those talks are amazing.

If you want to network in the context of ministry, you must:

- Meet as many people as you can.

- Look for people who are doing good.

- Act like a host, not a guest.

- Make friends even when you don't need to.

- Keep in touch. Everywhere you go, try to touch base with the people you know in that city.

- Developing a filing system.

- Serve before you receive.

- Follow up. (Most do not do this.)

Remember: Who you know is as important as what you know.

DOCUMENTATION

Write the vision, and make it plain upon tables, that he may run that readeth it.

~Hab. 2:2 KJV

At the Institute, The Summit, and Detroit Partnership, we have been careful to document every process, every principle, and every procedure so that others can learn from our experiences. This is so important. In order for leadership to continue from generation to generation, there must be a "how-to" record; otherwise, people start from square one every twenty to twenty-five years. Tragically, this "reinventing the wheel" has occurred all too often in the church.

The documentation must be written as a "blueprint," such that a novice can see clearly what they need to do in order to replicate a program, ministry or event. On our website, www.ifbfd.org, we have a section devoted to documentation that describes our ministries and events. My office is full of three-ringed binders with correspondence, forms, outlines, fact sheets, and ministry descriptions to ensure that the work continues after my generation has gone on to be with the Lord.

Every generation stands on the shoulders of the one before. Make sure that the generation after you is equipped to extend your ministry.

Remember what Jesus said: "Very truly, I tell *you*, whoever believes in me *will do* the works I have been doing, and they *will do* even *greater things* than these..." (John 14:12, emphasis mine).

While Jesus himself may not have left a written record, we benefit from the documents—Matthew, Mark, Luke, and John—that God inspired men of faith to write of his work, his methods, and his philosophy. We in ministry should follow that example.

SHARING

I was in a meeting with other ministry leaders. We were planning a major outreach/community service event, and I was explaining how all of the forms and correspondence we were using would be placed on our website. "Will you make that public?" some of them asked. "Yes," I said. They wondered why.

My answer: I believe strongly in the principle of multiplication. If I made that website accessible only to a few "insiders," I would limit the possibilities of ministry. The more we scatter, the more we share what we have and what we learned with others, the more extensively the gospel can be shared effectively throughout the earth. That's what's really important about sharing.

Matt Parker

KEY TO SUCCESS: RELINQUISHING CONTROL

The numbers I shared with you at the beginning of this chapter are just the tip of the iceberg. Summit members are now on virtually every continent with ministry activities. The Summit Group, however, is NOT in control of these activities. Our strategy is to provide information, grounding, and access to tools that allow individuals and ministries to flourish wherever the Lord leads them to go, with or without our specific input and direction. For us, that strategy has led to an explosion of international impact.

COUNTRIES SERVED

- **Africa**
  - » Benin, Ethiopia, Ghana, Ivory Coast, Mali, Nigeria, Uganda

- **Asia**
  - » Japan

- **Australia**
  - » Sydney

- **Europe**
  - » Budapest, Italy, London, Romania, Spain

- **North America**
  - » Florida, Georgia, Illinois, Maryland, Massachusetts, Michigan, Minnesota, Mississippi, Missouri, North Carolina, Ohio, Pennsylvania, Tennessee, Texas, Wisconsin

- **South America**
  - » Bahamas, Caribbean, Haiti, Jamaica

Right now, Summit Group members are directly or indirectly equipping more than one million people internationally, and impacting more than 500,000 leaders to engage in reproducing other leaders. They are doing that through direct ministry, support of or collaboration with other ministries, and publication and distribution of Christian books and pamphlets.

In the long term, The Summit will host annual worldwide Summits to reach pastors, families, men, women, and youth workers. We will also partner with ministry organizations, service organizations, and other institutions to sponsor our annual "Day of Outreach," an event that features provision of food, information, social service resources, and evangelistic outreach. The Summit will also partner with World Vision to extend their reach into urban centers; and with The National Campus Compact, an organization that integrates civic and community-based learning into the college curriculum.

The Summit will also make significant use of electronic and social media as well. We will ultimately distribute a newsletter updating our efforts to more than fifty thousand international Christian leaders, foundations, missions, and publishers. We will also begin a dialogue with the Ashoka Fellowship Movement, an organization that supports "social entrepreneurs" with innovative, bold ideas for significant social transformation.

The Summit Group represents one of the most effective forms of "Succession Leadership." We began with a group of Christian leaders who aspired to make a genuine impact. We provided them with ample opportunities for structured and unstructured interaction. We brought resources from established Christian institutions to the conference table. We then allowed the "sparks to fly" as Christian leaders of color interacted with each other and with predominantly white Christian institutions. In other words, we "seeded" the ministries with information, opportunities to collaborate, and a foundational philosophical perspective on cross-cultural collaborations that helped to ground the work going forward.

The result has been far greater than we could have imagined. We are grateful that we don't control the process.

I have planted, Apollos watered, but God gave the increase.

~1 Cor. 3:6 KJV

For more information on The Summit, visit www.ifbfd.org

Chapter 3

THE JOSHUA GENERATION: SECOND-GENERATION LEADERSHIP

Dolphus Weary

Joshua 1:6–9 introduces us to a pivotal point in the ministry of Joshua. The people of Israel were about to enter the Promised Land. Although there had been times of conflict during the forty-year journey since the exodus from Egypt, the people had learned to trust the leadership provided by Moses, the man of God. After Moses died, the reins of leadership were turned over to a younger man named Joshua. God gave Joshua a very necessary threefold encouragement for the task by saying,

> Be strong and courageous, because you will lead these people to inherit the land I swore to their ancestors to give them. Be strong and very courageous.... Have I not commanded you? Be strong and courageous. Do not be afraid; do not be discouraged, for the Lord your God will be with you wherever you go.
>
> ~Joshua 1:6–7, 9

THE INTIMIDATING MANTLE OF LEADERSHIP

From my own experience, I can imagine that young Joshua felt intimidated to be following in the footsteps of a person who had been as powerful—one whom he had held in such high esteem—as Moses. Now it was Joshua's time to lead the children of Israel to the next step.

I grew up in Mississippi without a father in my home. In 1964, shortly after becoming a Christian under the ministry of John Perkins, founder of Voice of Calvary, I became involved with the ministry in Mendenhall and began to regard Perkins as my spiritual dad. I saw him model servant leadership. John was a person who, in spite of his third-grade education, displayed all the earmarks of a man of God whose unselfish leadership would one day enable him to become the founding president of a holistic Christian movement that is spreading around the nation and even into other countries. Naturally I felt intimidated, as do many second-generation leaders who fear we cannot measure up to the standard established by the current leader.

EDUCATION AND TRAINING

After high school, I went on to junior college. When I talked to John one day in the middle of my sophomore year, he encouraged me to consider attending a Christian college. We looked at some colleges and found an interesting one in California by the name of L. A. Baptist College. John worked out a plan with the coach and the director of admissions to get me a basketball scholarship—fantastic support from a leader who had already done so much for our community.

The Need for Finances

After my first year in California, I came back during the summer of 1968 to find a job and stay at home with my family, only to face a reality that did not meet with my expectations. In rural Mendenhall, there were few jobs available for young people, and even fewer jobs for young Black males. After looking for a job for a number of days, I decided to go to Washington, D.C. My brother had told me that he could get me a job there. Two days prior to leaving Mendenhall, John Perkins and I talked about the possibility of developing our own ministry within the community so that young people like me would not always have to leave, but could look at the possibility of having something to which to come back.

I came back to Mendenhall with no money, just a dream and a vision. We started our first summer leadership development program, and I became the director with a staff of three young people. We offered a vacation Bible school service to rural churches. The churches opened their doors, and we provided the teaching and all materials at no cost. Little did I know that the process of leadership development was beginning to take place. For me, this project was an opportunity to experience the joy of having a father figure interested in my development as a person. In John's mind, it was doubtless a strategic move to groom me for leadership.

Strategic Leadership Development

Every ministry that wants to survive must pass on the vision to the second generation. These are the apprentices who will succeed the current leadership and carry the ministry to new heights. Owning the vision is very important, because a ministry often dies in the second or third generation if there is not a clear commitment to the original vision. I firmly believe that early on, John Perkins, in his role as the first-generation leader, wanted me to have a good understanding of the vision for something he called "Christian Community Development."

This became clear as I returned to work in the 1969 summer program. Realizing that racial integration was soon going to come to the public school system, we expanded our vacation Bible school by adding a tutorial program to provide our youth with adequate reading and math skills with which to face those new challenges. In addition, we added a Black history component because many of our young people did not have a healthy appreciation of who we are and from where we have come. I was given increased responsibility for running the programs.

Having graduated from college earlier that year, I contemplated going to seminary in the fall of 1969. By this time, I had made a definite commitment to be in some type of full-time Christian ministry but still had not made a commitment to return to Mississippi. Understanding first hand how racism and poverty had debilitated the Black community, my plan as a teenager was to go to college, get an education, and get out of Mississippi, as so many friends and family members had done.

A major change occurred in my thinking during May and June of 1970 while traveling with Overseas Crusade, Sports Ambassadors, and Ventures for Victory (a Christian basketball team).We played local teams and shared our faith in Taiwan, the Philippines, and Hong Kong in a missionary effort to use sports to reach the lost. While on that trip, Norm Cook, the coach, observed my leadership skills in dealing with the young Taiwanese and began to challenge me about becoming a full-time missionary under Overseas Crusade or Sports Ambassadors. I thought this was a great idea. I could be involved in missionary work without going back to Mississippi. Yet I responded, "Let's pray and see what God has to say." Six weeks and sixty-plus ball games later, to my surprise, I had to tell Norm that God was calling me back to Mississippi. God kept bringing this plaguing question to my mind: *What is going to happen to the people who are trapped in rural Mississippi if I don't return to help them?*

I returned to Mendenhall after my experience in the Orient and discussed my desire to return to Mendenhall with my future wife Rosie. She agreed that if this was God's call on my life, she would accept it as her call as well. We were married in August of 1970. At the time, I had one year of seminary remaining. Rosie had two years of college to go.

Didn't Want to Go Back

After my graduation from seminary in 1971, John Perkins presented me with a huge challenge. "Dolphus, if you are going to come back to Mendenhall to work with us, what I need you to do is go out and raise your support." This was another major hurdle for me to overcome. I wanted to get a job and earn a living for my family. I did not want to depend upon other people for my financial needs. Obviously, this was a hurdle God wanted me to face. So after returning to California for Rosie's senior year, we began the process of raising funds. A California church provided more than two thirds of our support. They helped us to see that God would provide.

Opportunity to Fail

I learned a lot during those summers of 1968, 1969, and 1970 in Mendenhall as I experienced the ups and downs of second generation leadership. I learned that the first generation must not only confer a leadership title and responsibility to the second generation, but must also give the power and authority to implement that leadership. It is much more difficult to pass the baton successfully if the leader-in-training has not had an opportunity to fail.

John was so interested in my success that he did everything possible to keep me from failing. But that approach worked against me. I never had a chance to grow up. I left Mendenhall a boy and came back a boy. Neither seminary nor the summer ministry had provided the kind of training and experience I needed to develop into the seasoned leader who would be ready to lead a growing ministry to our people.

The other challenge was the phenomenon typical of first-generation leaders of "authority yo-yo"—that is, giving authority and then taking it back to make sure the "right" decision is made. Even after I had been given the responsibility to run all the programs, John would step in and make decisions from time to time. I was once given an assistant who was given responsibility for my entire staff; but I had not been consulted in this decision. It was at such points that I felt like I was being treated as a boy rather than a man. Often I felt like going to some other ministry where I could exercise more of my gifts. Today, as I look back on the struggles and frustrations, I realize this was all a part of being a second-generation leader. I realize now that it is extremely difficult for a first-generation leader to let go. Perhaps, more importantly, no one had given John a road map to follow in developing a second-generation leader. He was going through his own on-the-job training.

Recommendations

Eventually, John decided to spin The Mendenhall Ministries off from its parent, Voice of Calvary. This was no doubt made with the best of intentions. However, it came across like a father trying to force his children to grow up; if the sons failed, they could always come back to their father for help. But because the sons were not involved in the original decision to get spun off, there arose a competitive desire to *prove to Dad* that we were not going to fail. The result was friction between leaders who both wanted to do God's will in serving our communities. Praise God, time and good communication have healed the hurts. Most of the pain could have been avoided, however, if there had been a clear understanding between the first-generation leader and the new leader. Many times, first-generation leaders view second generation leaders as sons or daughters. At some point the relationship needs to change from parent-child to mentor-protégé, and finally peer-to-peer.

So the question is: At what point do we clearly make a transition from the parent-child model with its accompanying paternalistic treatment? What is the right time to become peer partners and start working together? And how do we train our respective brains to *think* correctly during the transition, in order to reduce the possibility of friction and conflict?

Our experience suggests several recommendations for other ministries which are making long-range plans for leadership transfer. First af all, allow second-generation leaders to go away for a period of time to gain their own leadership style. Recognize that, more than likely, that style will be different from that of the present leader. However, the first generation leader must accept that leadership style. The context will no doubt have changed since the founding of the organization. Governments and other outside groups constantly introduce new challenges which affect the way the ministry will be carried out. The ministry will probably have grown in its impact. The backgrounds of the leaders will be different. The second-generation leader will have the advantage of standing on the shoulders of the first-generation leader. When you stand on someone else's shoulders, you can see farther— usually farther than the one on whose shoulders you stand.

After two decades of leading The Mendenhall Ministries, I am now faced with the same issues I once faced with my mentor John Perkins. I have now transitioned to a "first-generation" leader who has come face to face with the same challenges that my mentor had to confront. What to do is not nearly as simple as I used to think. After much prayer and counsel, here are some how-tos I have adopted to assist our second-generation leaders in developing their potential:

1. Begin *early* to give to second-generation persons a vision for coming back to the community.

2. Provide leadership opportunities for second-generation persons to grow and to develop.

3. Encourage second-generation leaders to go to some other place to work for one to three years in order to gain a greater sense of their own leadership skills and potential.

Dolphus Weary

4. Allow second-generation leaders to grow without looking over their shoulders all the time. Demonstrate confidence in emerging leaders as they begin to work in the ministry.

5. Agree to talk openly and often. One of the worst things that could happen would be not enough communication and affirmation occurring in both directions.

6. Allow your protégé the chance to fail.

Apprentice leaders need a lot of affirmation from the incumbent leader. They are often insecure in their leadership learning role, and nervous about the evaluation of their mentor. Nevertheless, it is important for the life of the vision that the organization work to grow new leaders. New individuals can take hold of and pursue the vision with vigor. A fantastic way to grow vision and commitment is to begin early to shape the second and third generations.

To solidify the competence of the next generation, the first-generation leader must incorporate structure. Joshua, the leader-to-be, no doubt observed Moses in many different situations, but it was a totally different experience when Joshua took over the reins and had to be the leader himself. Joshua needed the structure of the Law to inform and guide his leadership. That was just as important as the time he spent with Moses.

I, too, was challenged to take the leadership reins from John Perkins, a man whose intellect and dedication awed me. Here are a few steps to effect a smooth leadership transition:

1. Both parties should agree on the way the transition will take place.

2. Both parties should follow the agreed-upon plan.

3. Each person should express regular affirmation and commitment to the other.

4. Allow the first-generation leader to transition out slowly, to ensure that they continue to provide advice and perspective well into the leadership of the next generation. There is a delicate balance here,

but it is extremely important for the first generation to maintain continuity even as they pass on the mantle of leadership.

A partnership relationship should be formed so that the former leader knows that he can make recommendations to the new leader. The new leader must also know that he has not only freedom to make decisions, but also the freedom to go to the first generation for advice—as well as the authority to decide whether to follow that advice.

I learned a number of things from my experience over the last twenty years.

1. Leadership is not easy for either the first-generation leader or the apprentice leader.

2. It is easier to analyze how things should have been done than to do everything right on a day-to-day basis. I like the one-liner which says, "When you are up to your armpits in alligators, it is difficult to remember that your original objective was to drain the swamp."

3. Nobody gave our pioneers a manual on leadership development. They had to create their own rules as they went along. It is a credit to their reliance on God that they have done so well.

4. Leadership training should be a more prominent part of college and seminary programs. This should include how to develop apprentices as well.

5. Problems can help in your development, even as the Bible says in James 1.

6. It is important for the second-generation leader to express what his expectations are, too, so that there can be a meeting of the minds on important issues. Differing unspoken assumptions can lead to confusion.

7. The first-generation leader is more open to suggestions than we sometimes think.

Dolphus Weary

At its base, leadership development is essentially discipleship. It takes place formally, but also informally, as the second generation walks alongside the first generation to learn strategies and tactics. The second-generation leader should learn as they go, be given gradual authority as they prove themselves mature, and allowed the opportunity to learn from failure. That is the next great challenge to my generation as we pass the baton to the next.

For more information on Weary, visit www.realchristianfoundation.info.

Chapter 4

CASE STUDIES IN SUCCESSION

Matt Parker, Sabrina Black, Michael and Maria Westbrook

THE GENERALS

(Matt Parker, Institute for Black Family Development)

Tom Skinner's vision of a succession of leadership started in 1999, with a selection of African American men to share his life with a group called "The Generals." The Generals met each year for fellowship, coaching, and networking with each other.

One of the group's goals was to select, mentor, and resource a new succession of leaders for the next generation. Even though Tom Skinner and Herman Heade are no longer alive, Harold Brinkley, Glandian Carney, Carl Ellis, Elward Ellis, Tom Fritz, Russell Knight, and Matthew Parker have developed churches and Christian nonprofits to accomplish this goal.

Matthew Parker's vehicle for a succession of leadership was an expanded version of the Generals program, started in 2009 in Detroit, Michigan. Other organizations are now also modeling the program in Minneapolis and Newark, New Jersey.

Roots

When Matthew Parker was still a child, his mother, Ruth Parker, died and left his father, Matt Parker, with two children to raise alone. Their father provided for their development until 1971, when he also passed away. Matthew Parker found himself turning to three special individuals: Barbara Walton, Lloyd Blue, and Tom Skinner. He asked them to be his spiritual parents and mentors. Fortunately for him, they agreed. He has been blessed.

These three people taught Parker much, and he always said that one day he would pay his debt to them by taking on a group of young people to provide the same kind of guidance and support he was so generously given.

Parker's version of "The Generals" originally started in 1993 as a pilot program called "The Executive Club," with thirty-five eighth- and ninth-graders. Parker approached a number of churches and asked if he could take on a group of young people to mentor and nurture spiritually.

They met on Saturdays from 9 a.m. to 2 p.m., brought in professionals and leaders to speak about many topics, included a time for Bible study, and frequently took the young people on field trips to area universities. They engaged them in service projects and initiatives where they could discover and hone their skills and talents.

Of that group of thirty-five, twenty-eight finished the four-year program and twenty-three went to college.

Enhancing on "The Executive Club" pilot, Parker received a four-year grant of $10,000.00 from The Comerica Charitable Foundation to start "The Neighborhood College." The Great Lakes Christian Foundation became a funder in 2009.

In 2009, Parker changed the name of the group from "The Neighborhood College" to "The Generals"—a nod to changing times and changing ideas of what would be expected and revered.

The educational status of African American teenagers is seen by many as a national emergency. On the average, nearly one third of all high school students drop out before graduation. In some cities, the percentage is significantly higher. The Detroit Chapter of the Michigan Association of Black Social Workers reported that eight percent of all jobs were available to high school dropouts. In the future, three percent of all jobs will be available to those without high-school diplomas. The fact that youth do not pursue post-secondary education in greater numbers is a severe problem that demands immediate attention.

The Generals believes that leadership is a learned art, a behavior that when learned, helps to create a new sense of reality, a new sense of purpose, and an engagement of dialogue with family, community, and society. It is in this context that the work with African Americans ages thirteen and above has been developed.

The Generals has been established to develop a comprehensive strategy for long-term participation into the lives of young people in the African American society.

The Generals is providing an empowering education with faculty who are professionals, scholars, and mentors. The Generals is committed to giving the tools, experiences, and relationships that will prepare future leaders with character.

Purpose

To provide a non-traditional academic leadership program designed for African-Americans ages thirteen and over for college, entrepreneurship, and leadership in the future.

Mission

To provide classroom experiences, networking, practical experiences, field trips, and mentors for African-Americans who are looking for role models they can trust.

Goals

- The Generals will learn how to make informed decisions regarding college enrollment and how to achieve success in college.

- The Generals will learn responsibility towards themselves, their family, and society.

- The Generals will develop a working knowledge of fundamentals of employment training, particularly in the areas of writing resumes, finding jobs, interviewing for employment, and interacting with potential employers.

- The Generals will acquire a basic working knowledge of how to succeed in business by developing and writing a logical, organized, and credible career plan.

- The Generals will be exposed to a comprehensive mentoring program designed to enhance their leadership skills for the commercial world, the realm of business, trade, and economics.

In order to achieve these, the Generals will be given a safe place to go during non-school hours. This is important in our communities; with a plethora of working two-parent and single-parent families, the hours between about 3 p.m. and 7 p.m. on weekdays, and even weekends, are especially fraught with risk as our children engaged in unsupervised, unmonitored activity. During these times, they will be exposed to college preparatory activities and the key elements of wise decision-making. These activities would effect a stronger connection to community as well as the marketplace; and their tendency to engage in more positive behaviors will also connect them to their families in a meaningful way.

The Generals will equip, network, and resource parents and students in the art of leadership, college preparation, and career development. The training program offers students a "how to" tap a full range of resources and develop a process for leadership development.

The program offers each year ten months of courses on one Saturday of each month, from 10:00 a.m. to 1:00 p.m. A key feature of the curriculum is building teamwork and partnerships. As a graduation requirement, students will design and implement a "Teen Summit" to share best practices and lessons learned to their peers.

For more information, visit www.ifbfd.org.

GIRLS WITH GREAT POTENTIAL

(Sabrina Black, Cofounder with Pamela Hudson, Girls with Great Potential)

"I want to pass on to girls the ability to live the abundant life."

In 2006, my partner Pamela Hudson and I founded Global Projects for Hope, Help and Healing (GPH3) with a commitment to reach unreached people around the world and to provide hope, help, and healing to those most vulnerable. We have been overwhelmed by the need we see around the world among women who are hurting, oppressed, brutalized, and in need of spiritual, economic, emotional, and psychological undergirding.

At some point, we made a decision to bring some of our work home, in our own country. Young African American women are in need of some of the same nurturing, love, and education that we have found ourselves giving to women from First, Second, and Third World countries. We developed a twelve-month series of meetings for Detroit-area girls aged eight to twelve (and eight- to sixteen-year-old girls internationally), and launched "Girls with Great Potential" to impart critical spiritual, physical, social, and intellectual skills.

Our mission is to particularly reach out to inner-city young girls, especially those who may have only one parent in the home or are being raised by their grandparents. We have high expectations of ourselves, and of our girls: we seek no less than to offer them hope, wholeness, and possibilities as they learn to make wise decisions. We seek to engage their critical-thinking skills and pique their interest in learning about themselves and others around the world. This is a global society, and to keep our girls tethered to where they live when the world is open to them is simply irresponsible.

We address seven key areas that allow girls to esteem themselves and empower them to a greater appreciation of the world around them and the possibilities it contains:

1. Global Citizenship—World Perspective. Understanding a global community, having a global consciousness and developing a global vision with a greater appreciation for cultural diversity, missions and geography. In this module, we encourage the girls to learn

one new language, especially our U.S. girls. The four languages we currently teach are Spanish, French, Japanese, and Arabic. Learning another country's language enlarges us to others and opens us to different ways of thinking. It is true: languages are a barometer for how a people group thinks about themselves and the world. Those who are in other countries learn two or more languages as a matter of course. We owe it to our girls to push them to do the same.

2. Cultural Heritage—Our girls need to know—and value—who they are. We expose our girls to their heritage as African American women, and we show them how to discover their own personal heritage and legacy by helping them document their family tree. We ask them two key questions: *Who are you? Where did you come from?* The girls then go back to their parents and interview them about their backgrounds, education and careers.

3. Health and Fitness—We emphasize better nutrition and eating habits, the benefits of exercise, physical activity, sleep, and finally, hygiene. Our family structures and work responsibilities have reduced or eliminated the time that families spend together at the breakfast or dinner table, and our overreliance on fast and other prepared foods has devastated our nutritional profiles. For many of our girls, the basics are not so basic.

4. Entrepreneur and Leadership Development—We know that those young people who will be successful will have to have a strong set of skills that respond to the new reality of uncertain job prospects, necessity for multiple streams of income, and the possibility that the current safety nets may not be in place when our girls become adults. In addition to exposure to more conventional career options and opportunities, we also show our girls how to start businesses, create a business plan, build dreams, network, and innovate. We provide critical money management skills that, again, they often do not get at home. We find that these exposures give girls a vision of what they can be. They actually dream bigger once they learn what is possible.

Matt Parker, Sabrina Black, Michael and Maria Westbrook

5. Educational Enrichment—Promoting academic excellence through our "Reading Marathon" with a list of books to prompt thirty minutes of reading per day helps to spur interest in reading, which helps our girls as they "find their voices" through public speaking training. We help close the technology gap with exposure to the latest technologies and gadgets; and our "Aspire Higher" project provides study and note-taking skills. Depending on their cultural context, we also teach practical trade skills such as sewing, cooking, catering, crafts, and cosmetology.

6. Social Skills and Etiquette—This represents another area where girls find themselves less able to navigate. The basic social graces are no longer obvious; saying "please" and "thank you" seems to be a lost art. We have recreated the old-fashioned "charm school" with advice on how to stand and sit properly, set a table and eat in public. Our "Fashion Police" segment addresses, with humor, how to make a good first impression. We finish this segment with advice on "How to be a Good Friend." Strong friendships with like-minded peers are critical to individual and group success.

7. Self-Esteem and Peer Pressure—Self-esteem does not occur in a vacuum. Foundational to self-esteem is character building. We have incorporated a "Building Character and Integrity" segment into this module. With character in place, we turn our attention to body images and the dangers of comparing oneself with others. We also cover the basics of dating and relationships, with an emphasis on domestic violence. Finally, we explore the dangers of substance abuse (alcohol and drugs) and premarital sex, emphasizing the power of abstinence in both areas.

But our work is not confined to the classroom. We believe in the discipleship model, which calls for walking alongside the girls in an extended family relationship and integrating the lessons learned in formal instruction. Our Tea Party allows us to "walk out" the lessons of friendship and etiquette. Our "Blue Jean Craft Event" lets us interact informally while working on a project—one of the best ways to learn leadership and relationship skills. Our Summer Luau exposes the girls to other cultures in a non-academic, fun setting. This combination of classroom learning and informal mentoring in a fun, festive setting allows the girls to learn from us as well as from each other, and gives them ample opportunities to "walk out" what they've learned in an environment that is nurturing and welcoming.

Our motto is "Calling Forth Greatness from the Children of Promise." We repeat over and over to the girls that they are children of promise. More importantly, we show them what that means by helping them discover heritage, hope, and a great future.

Your help has made me great.

~Ps. 18:35

For more information, visit www.globalprojects.org.

METROPOLITAN URBAN LEADERSHIP INSTITUTE (MULI)—A MINISTRY OF GREATER LIFE, INC.

(Revs. Michael and Maria Westbrook, Copastors, Greater Life, Inc.)

The Greater Life story started 25 years ago, when Reverends Michael and Maria Westbrook decided to do something about a troubling paradigm among Newark's after-school and summer enrichment programs: The majority of these services were not available to the young men and women who needed them most. Kids with gang affiliations or truancy records were usually not permitted to attend afterschool programs; only those with clean records were allowed to participate. However, in Newark's South Ward, where Greater Life began and still operates today, there is a particular need for targeted services for this population: the region's poverty epidemic has spawned a culture of gang violence, drug trade, and spiritual alienation.

To successfully reach those at-risk youth of color disqualified by other after-school programs, we have spent a quarter of a century developing and perfecting programs that balance cultural sensitivity, inspiration, and moral focus to turn thousands of Greater Life kids into more productive members of society. Throughout, they have operated on the principle that, if given the opportunity, every young man and woman, regardless of their background or personal history, has the capacity to focus their talents and energy towards positive growth. Greater Life affords its students this opportunity by offering a welcoming, nurturing alternative to the threatening aspects of inner-city culture. We have built Greater Life into more than a disconnected set of homework help and camping programs—it is instead a community of support in which every new student in assigned a mentor from our staff and alumni, and with which poor and at-risk students grow from grade school, through high school, into a successful adulthood.

OUR MISSION

Greater Life's mission is to educate and inspire at-risk and behaviorally challenged youth with innovative and culturally-sensitive programs, so they may thrive academically, socially, and morally. The organization was formally incorporated as a charitable non-profit 501(c)(3) Faith-Based Community Youth & Family Organization in 2003. It previously operated as a subsidiary of the national non-profit Young Life. We have effectively served more than fifteen thousand young people, caregivers, and family members.

Greater Life is dedicated to reaching and serving Newark's indigent, poor, disadvantaged, or at risk youth—and their families—on a daily basis. The Greater Life program site is located in a 5,000-square-foot mixed-use space at 272 Chancellor Avenue, centrally located in Newark's South Ward and situated directly across the street from Weequahic High School and Chancellor Avenue Grade School, two of our primary public-school partners. Greater Life is easily accessible by public transportation and the facility itself is wheelchair accessible. We also plan to acquire the 2,200-square-foot space directly adjacent to our building with the goal of using it to house our expanded Kidstitute program.

Through longstanding partnerships and community collaborators, we offer camping experiences and summer trips that offer Newark students subsidized opportunities to get out of the city. Our program focus is designed to promote improved grades and behavior, peak physical health, productive social skills, improved interpersonal behavior, strong moral standards, improved family connections, community involvement, and volunteerism.

OUR CLIENTS

Every year, Greater Life provides services to fifteen hundred youth ages seven to nineteen, and their family members, targeting those affected by poverty, with unstable family lives, and at risk of being influenced by gangs and the drug culture. This group is tragically growing due in large part to Newark's poverty epidemic: One in three Newark children grow up in poverty. Essex County has the unfortunate distinction of possessing the third highest level of severe poverty in New Jersey: 6.3 percent of Essex families were living at less than fifty percent of the federal poverty rate in 2008, compared to one percent in the most affluent county in New Jersey (Somerset) and four percent statewide. The child poverty rate in Essex County is also third highest in the state. In 2008, when the state child poverty rate was at 12.5 percent and the national average leapt to 18.2 percent as a result of the recent economic downturn, the rate in Essex County rose to an alarming 20.2 percent.

The consequences of Newark's poverty epidemic are severe:

- Every week, eleven infants are born to adolescents.

- Less than fifty percent of eighth graders pass the state proficiency tests every year, and nearly twenty-eight children are removed from their homes every week as a result of suspected abuse or neglect.

- More than one-quarter of Newark high-school seniors fail to graduate every year.

- From 2000 to 2004, school violence incidents in Newark involving weapons jumped eighty-four percent.

- From 2000 to 2004, the amount of grandparents forced to raise their grandchildren leapt seventy-three percent.

We are blessed to lead a dedicated staff, a corps of consultants and volunteers, and a board of directors that knows Newark and its surrounding communities, particularly the South Ward, intimately. In many cases, Greater Life alumni return to serve as mentors or volunteers. The leader of our Kidstitute educational enrichment program is Annette Alston, the president of the Newark Teachers' Association.

Why is it important to have a staff that knows the neighborhood well? Because the staff finds the kids that need our help most by walking the streets, and by visiting basketball courts and playgrounds daily to identify and immediately assist these children and teenagers who are often in crisis situations.

The Next Level

In 1996, we decided that we needed to establish a more formal way to develop the leadership skills of our alumni mentors and volunteers. We birthed the Metropolitan Urban Leadership Institute (MULI) to identify, hire, train, and equip the very youth that we seek to serve. These are the young people who have been overlooked, criminalized, and locked out by mainstream society. That, for us, was paramount; the best people to mentor and lead marginalized young people are...other marginalized young people. We are now working to reach forty students per calendar year. These students will be highly trained in a two-year program that will cover:

- *Mentoring*—We will provide mentors from ministry and secular occupations at a 5:1 (student: mentor) ratio.

- *Leadership Development*—We will help students identify their gifts, talents and abilities and help students establish individual plans of action.

- *Program Development*—We will show students how to manage, execute, and evaluate the various programs of Greater Life. They will be intimately involved in helping us plan and run the Annual "Teen Impact" retreat that hosts more than 450 attendees; and the above-mentioned "Kidstitute Education Enrichment Program." They will also be taught in our Duke's Café Entrepreneurial Training After Program Center; this new coffee/snack shop facility is student-run. Students will develop critical math skills in real-life applications as they plan and evaluate budgets and take inventory. They channel their artistic instincts as they design and decorate the shop, and they will be challenged to make executive decisions about the best way to manage the shop overall.

- *Fundraising*—Students will gain a rich set of skills by involvement here. They will learn to write effective fundraising letters; they will learn math applications as they develop and determine budgets; and learn decision-making as they experience the consequences of the decisions they make.

- *Office Administration*—Students will learn the rudiments of running an office. They'll work on the computer, help organize files, and answer, with supervision, email and "snail mail" correspondence. Again, the elements of success are there: oral and written communications, file organization, personal communications, and customer service.

- *Community Engagement/Networking*—students will go with our leadership to various community functions. We believe it is important to expose them to the environment in which they operate, and to establish critical community connections that make them viable members of the sphere in which they operate. We make our students visible.

As they do the important work of helping in the ministry, our students become significant to themselves and to our community. We are excited about these efforts to pass down our leadership to the next generation.

You have heard me teach things that have been confirmed by many reliable witnesses. Now teach these truths to other trustworthy people who will be able to pass them on to others.

~2 Tim. 2:2 NLT

For more information, visit www.greaterlifenewark.org.

PART TWO: LIVING PRINCIPLES

Walking out the Call to Leadership

Chapter 5

EFFECTIVE CHURCH LEADERSHIP

Paul Cannings

The absolute foundation for developing church ministry must rest on the authority of the Word of God. Leaders are therefore guided and directed as a result of the principles outlined in scripture. Because Christ is the head of the church (Eph. 1:22), leaders must function under His headship in order to facilitate God's plans, purpose, and will for the church (Eph. 1:11). Leaders do not have to develop principles by which to guide the church, these principles are already outlined and they stand as the authority for God's church.

A leader is someone who is more committed to the call for service than anyone else around him/her. Each leader must recognize that there is a day of accountability for the service they did provide or the service they provided incorrectly (James 3:1; Matt. 25:14–30). Leaders will account for the work done in the flesh (1 Cor. 3:10–15; 2 Cor. 5:10).

> *Therefore, my beloved brethren, be steadfast, immovable, always abounding in the work of the Lord, knowing that your toil is not in vain in the Lord.*
>
> ~1 Cor. 15:58 NASB

As we consider the succession of leadership, we should first define what a good leader looks like from a biblical perspective.

THE BIBLICAL NATURE OF AN EFFECTIVE LEADER:

The Son of Man came not to be ministered unto, but to minister.
~Mark 10:45 KJV

I have set you an example that you should do as I have done for you.
~John 13:15

In the words of James Means, "Leaders in the church exist to facilitate the ministry of the whole body; they are not appointed to dominate or control the body."[1]

First and foremost, Christian leaders are servants (Matt. 20:27–28; Mark 10:44–45; Phil. 2:5–7). Jesus Christ spoke with a servant's heart. Secondly, each leader's service is first determined by their spiritual gift.

Each of you should use whatever gift you have received to serve others, as faithful stewards of God's grace in its various forms.
~1 Peter 4:10

Leaders should not serve in areas where God has not gifted them. If leaders serve in an area outside of their giftedness, they serve in their own strength and outside the will of God.

A LEADER MUST BE A GOOD STEWARD.

This, then, is how you ought to regard us: as servants of Christ and as those entrusted with the mysteries God has revealed. Now it is required that those who have been given a trust must prove faithful.
~1 Cor. 4:1–2

The Matthew 25 story of the talents (vss. 14–46) says it all. Those who made good use of what the master gave them were given more resources; the one who hid his talents had even that taken away. See also Acts 20:28; Col. 1:25, 28; 1 Thess. 2:7, 12; 1 Tim. 1:14; 3:1; Titus 1:7; and 1 Peter 2:25.

---

1. James E. Means, *Leadership in Christian Ministry* (Grand Rapids, MI: Baker, 1989), 47..

A LEADER MUST BE A TRUE DISCIPLE OF CHRIST.

Now great multitudes went with Him. And He turned and said to them, "If anyone comes to Me and does not hate his father and mother, wife and children, brothers and sisters, yes, and his own life also, he cannot be My disciple. And whoever does not bear his cross and come after Me cannot be My disciple. For which of you, intending to build a tower, does not sit down first and count the cost, whether he has enough *to finish* it—*lest, after he has laid the foundation, and is not able to finish, all who see* it *begin to mock him, saying, "This man began to build and was not able to finish"? Or what king, going to make war against another king, does not sit down first and consider whether he is able with ten thousand to meet him who comes against him with twenty thousand? Or else, while the other is still a great way off, he sends a delegation and asks conditions of peace. So likewise, whoever of you does not forsake all that he has cannot be My disciple.*

~Luke 14:25–33 NKJV

A LEADER MUST BE MORE COMMITTED
TO THE WORD OF GOD THAN TRADITION.

As you therefore have received Christ Jesus the Lord, so walk in Him, rooted and built up in Him and established in the faith, as you have been taught, abounding in it with thanksgiving. Beware lest anyone cheat you through philosophy and empty deceit, according to the tradition of men, according to the basic principles of the world, and not according to Christ.

~Col. 2:6–8 NKJV; also see Matt. 15:2–9

A LEADER IS A FOLLOWER... OF CHRIST.

And Jesus, walking by the Sea of Galilee, saw two brothers, Simon called Peter, and Andrew his brother, casting a net into the sea; for they were fishermen. Then He said to them, "Follow Me, and I will make you fishers of men." They immediately left their *nets and followed Him.*

~Matt. 4:18–20 NKJV

A LEADER MUST BE COMMITTED
TO THE AUTHORITY OF SCRIPTURE.

All Scripture is given by inspiration of God, and is profitable for doctrine, for reproof, for correction, for instruction in righteousness, that the man of God may be complete, thoroughly equipped for every good work.

~2 Tim. 3:16–17 NKJV

A LEADER DEMONSTRATES A
DEPENDENCY ON THE HOLY SPIRIT.

Not that we are sufficient of ourselves to think of anything as being from ourselves, but our sufficiency is from God, who also made us sufficient as ministers of the new covenant, not of the letter but of the Spirit; for the letter kills, but the Spirit gives life.

~2 Cor. 3:5–6 NKJV

Leaders must recognize their insufficiency, and their need for the work of the Holy Spirit through Christ, before they can ever be totally effective. See also: Moses in Exodus 3:11–12; Numbers 11:16–17; Gideon in Judges 6:15; Jeremiah in Jeremiah 1:6; Paul in 2 Corinthians 12:9–10; 2 Timothy 3:17. The effective leader actually *models the fruit of the Spirit* before the congregation.

But the fruit of the Spirit is love, joy, peace, forbearance, kindness, goodness, faithfulness, gentleness and self-control. Against such things there is no law.

~Gal. 5:22–23

A LEADER MAKES DISCIPLES.

Christ did not tell the disciples to make leaders first. He instructed them to make disciples before anything else can be established within the church.

Therefore go and make disciples of all nations, baptizing them in the name of the Father and of the Son and of the Holy Spirit...

~Matt. 28:19

An effective leader has a team spirit. A person who does the work of the Lord must recognize that he is a part of a body, working with other believers so that body grows spiritually, and shares Christ with others (Eph. 4:12–13, 16). When the world sees the church working together as a team, they witness the validity of our faith.

A LEADER MUST HAVE INTEGRITY.

But you, man of God, flee from all this, and pursue righteousness, godliness, faith, love, endurance and gentleness. Fight the good fight of the faith. Take hold of the eternal life to which you were called when you made your good confession in the presence of many witnesses. In the sight of God, who gives life to everything, and of Christ Jesus, who while testifying before Pontius Pilate made the good confession, I charge you to keep this *command without spot or blame until the appearing of our Lord Jesus Christ...*

~1 Tim. 6:11–14

See also Exodus 18:21; Matthew 18:16; Philippians 2:14–15 ; 1 Timothy 3:3, 8, 11; and 2 Timothy 2:2.

ADDITIONAL IMPORTANT LEADERSHIP CHARACTERISTICS

- A leader must be teachable and reliable (2 Tim. 2:2, 15).

- A leader must not be argumentative (Prov. 17:19; 1 Tim. 6:3–5; 2 Tim. 2:14, 24).

- A leader must have the mindset of Jesus Christ (Phil. 2:1–5; Col. 3:1–4).

- A leader must be flexible (Acts 16:6 ; 1 Cor. 16:6–7; 2 Cor. 1:15–17).

- A leader must be thorough (Matt. 28:19–20; John 17:4, 8; Col. 1:27–28).

- A leader does not run from challenges (1 Cor. 16:9; 2 Cor. 4:10).

- A leader must work for oneness (John 17:20–23), and take action against those who create division (Romans 16:17–18; 2 Thess. 3:14–15; Titus 3:9–11).

- A leader must be willing to take the initiative. Think about Jesus washing the disciples' feet in John 13; or Paul gathering wood after a shipwreck in Acts 27. The leader who takes the initiative will act when there is an issue that needs to be resolved between two believers (Matt. 5:23–24; 18:15), or to secure the information they need (Prov. 20:5), or to set and achieve goals.

A man's heart plans his way, But the Lord directs his steps.

~Prov. 16:9 NKJV

EFFECTIVE LEADERSHIP SKILLS THAT MATTERS MOST

In addition to the character qualities listed above, an effective leader must have a knowledge base in the areas of planning, organizing, directing, staffing, and motivating. They must be able to stimulate followers to grow spiritually, allowing their individual relationships to God empower and inform their enthusiasm for the work of the ministry. They must know how to engage followers in plan formation and execution; when followers have ownership, they also have responsibility. They must concentrate on vision, cheerleading, and teaching rather than get bogged down in the details. Finally, they must show gratefulness to the people who are carrying out the work, to energize them to continue.

CONCLUSION

As leaders, we can become busy doing a lot of things that may or may not be effective. However, if we are not growing spiritually and developing a personal walk with God, all that we are doing will soon become frustrating, and meaningless (1 Cor. 3:12–15). We must first focus on our own spiritual development, and personal relationship with God before anything else can truly be a blessing for His kingdom and our lives. Christ's first focus was the spiritual development of His disciples, then came the training for effective leadership. When spiritual growth is the focus, effective leadership can thrive.

If anyone builds on this foundation using gold, silver, costly stones, wood, hay or straw, their work will be shown for what it is, because the Day will bring it to light. It will be revealed with fire, and the fire will test the quality of each person's work. If what has been built survives, the builder will receive a reward.

~1 Cor. 3:12–14

For more information, visit www.lwfellowshipchurch.org.

Chapter 6

FROM PASTOR TO TEAM

Russell Knight

A t one time, immense changes in technology demanded that America move from transportation by horse to a new mode of travel called the automobile. At the beginning of this new experiment, many supporters of the faithful horse were not easily convinced. They knew the worth and value of the horse, but the automobile was a brand-new concept.

The style of pastoral leadership in the African American church, going back even into the period of slavery, has almost always been dictated by the times. An enslaved people and those recently liberated required a "take-charge" leader. For that reason, the predominant type was an authoritarian "Moses" to lead his people to the promised land.

As the pastor, he was the one who possessed the vision, spoke for his people and the community, was an outstanding orator and preacher, was seemingly a magician in administrative matters, and for the most part, operated within the realm of selective accountability. That simply meant that the pastor was a law unto himself and could only be held accountable as he chose to allow himself to be.

Whole congregations grew to be totally dependent upon an individual who, during the slavery and post-slavery eras, has been described as perhaps the most essential person in the African American community. The importance of the Moses type of leader cannot be minimized. This style of leadership was highly successful and should be credited in large part with the survival of a people in the midst of severe crisis.

Whatever the critics may say, it is doubtful that African Americans would have accomplished as much without the vital leadership provided by these godly, and often legendary, men. It is interesting, nevertheless, that even though the church was born, and developed in the New Testament, supporters of the Moses style of leadership almost never use the New Testament to justify that style. They go instead to Old Testament leadership models that predate the church. This is reasonable since the slave church equated its struggle with that of Israel in the Old Testament. In that context, Moses spoke for God and carried the vision.

In order to fully comprehend the where-are-we question, we must at least acknowledge that after the civil rights era, many changes began to take place in the African American church, just as many changes began to transpire in society at large. One of these changes had to do with the increased education and competency level of the laity. No longer was the pastor the best educated individual in the community and the church. Better job training and better positions in the workplace slowly helped created lay persons who were highly skilled in the very things that were formerly done at the church by pastors. The outside community began to look to others as spokespeople for African Americans based on their competence to speak intelligently on a wealth of topics.

More and more, on their jobs, African Americans were trained to manage people, set budgets, hire personnel, advertise, raise funds, build buildings, and coordinate programs. Not only this, but in many churches, laypersons were also attending Bible schools and seminaries in order to enhance their lives spiritually. Soon, it became obvious that biblical knowledge was not something that only pastors could pursue.

While in many quarters, charisma alone seemed enough on which to get by, other pastors struggled to find ways to lead such enlightened memberships. Churches began questioning the concept of a Moses-style leadership and started trying to find whether or not something called "team" might be more applicable to today's African American church.

In fact, newer congregations have already begun exploring the idea of multiple leadership (two or more pastors or other staff). They are no longer looking to find "a" pastor who preaches, teaches, visits, counsels, administers, manages, and speaks for his congregation. Believing that all churches have several members with pastoral gifts, they are prepared to encourage more leadership at the top.

The question of "Which kind of leadership style is needed in the church today?" is not a criticism of what happened successfully in the past. The question is whether that which worked in the past will carry us through the difficult days ahead, or whether we need to encourage a different style—one which will better meet our needs while releasing for service many of the laypersons in our churches who are severely underused.

Today's church must have leadership with a holistic view of mission and the gifts to answer some of the social ills of our communities as it continues to evangelize. Therefore, more and more church leaders are participating in community development projects and working on such problems as housing and jobs.

Under the style of leadership that we call "team," the senior pastor is much more of a team player and coach. This does not mean that there is no longer a place for "the buck to stop," but it does mean that we can no longer have one individual who feels obligated to make independent decisions that impact others. The new "player/coach" is not intimidated by differing points of view or differing personality types. In fact, he understands that this can be a great advantage in team building.

Many congregations continue to call pastors who can provide them with a Moses style of leadership, while others feel it necessary to try something different. I see this desire for change as a positive direction for many churches, but I don't think that every church has to move immediately to the new while the old still works.

One of the oft-stated criticisms of the Moses style of leadership is that it does not easily embrace change. Newer churches recognize that ways must be found to reach the unsaved and unchurched, which may include such matters as helping them to find work and restoring to some a sense of dignity and worth.

Successful churches will eventually investigate the concept of "team" and stop asking an individual to pastor in the traditional sense of the word. They will recognize the fact that no one person can give them all that they desire and need in leadership.

Jethro advised Moses that it would be wiser and more effective to use a team in the accomplishing of the ministry. Moses did the right thing. He listened, and the results were outstanding. It is important to see that Moses had some of the same negative conditions that today's church leaders face. He had to contend with murmurings and conflict (Exod. 16–17), and yet he succeeded. Once he learned how to organize and use the abilities of others, the ministry prospered.

Although the church certainly is not a business, it must be more businesslike in its operation. In the concept of "team," excellence is promoted, accountability is enlarged, ownership is shared, and creativity is encouraged, thereby enabling the entire church to make better use of natural leaders.

It is important to note that there are few models of "team" leadership in the African American church at this point in time. Those who defend the Moses style of leadership have the weight of tradition on their side and use it to almost deify what worked in the past. While I, too, agree that it was invaluable in its time, that style of leadership blocks the development of other leaders and, therefore, denies the church a total concept of leadership.

Churches that choose to try the team approach to leadership will find it difficult to learn from others. Most people have only been exposed to one style of leadership in the church, so the models of other styles are few or nonexistent. We are desperately in need of those who will pioneer a new way, who will become models to churches which anxiously look for better ways to encourage leadership development. So, simply asking the question, "Where else is this being tried?" does not solve the problem.

Without a doubt, the concept of team leadership is biblical. *Moses* developed a team, *Jesus* used a team to accomplish his goals, *Elijah* selected *Elisha* to help him, and the *early church* enlarged its team to reach its goals.

Today's leaders must not attempt to lead individually or in isolation, nor should they be obsessed with empire building. Instead, God is looking for leaders who will humbly serve as part of a team which supplements and encourages one another. This kind of team, fully accountable, can mobilize the church in the days ahead.

In order to create an effective team ministry, the following suggestions are valuable:

MISSION AND PURPOSE

Many churches and parachurch organizations have a difficult time identifying their mission and purpose. However, it is important to be able to start right if you hope to end right. Actually, by answering two very simple questions, you can discover your organization's mission and purpose. Those questions are (1) What will we be doing? and (2) Why will we be doing it?

As a consultant to churches, parachurch organizations, and small businesses, I have found that it is not uncommon for the answers to these two questions to be hazy and unclear. Even though there is a mission or purpose statement in the constitution or charter of an organization, few who are connected know what those documents actually contain.

The *process* that creates the mission statement is as important as the actual answers to the questions. In other words, it is critical to have the right people in the room when the mission statement is being formed and that they all have something to do with creating what everyone can "own."

When an organization has a clear mission statement which comes from contributions by everyone in the group, the entire team will be motivated around this "vision." However, when the mission is passed on by the boss, board, or a limited subset of those who have a vested interest, then there is often a problem in motivation and ownership.

While staying at the Hampton Inn in Colorado Springs, the most prominent thing I saw posted at the registration desk and in the elevator was the mission statement of that organization. I was impressed with the quality of the service I received there. The management informed me that the entire hotel staff had participated in the process of forming the mission statement.

It is a good idea to find ways of constantly reminding everyone on the team of their mission and to have periodic evaluations which tell how well you are doing.

Finally, it becomes necessary every now and then to update these statements. With the passing of time and the changing of leadership and personnel, it is not unusual for missions and purposes to change. It is important to stay current.

TEAM MEMBER PROFILE

Develop a desired profile for discussion with potential team members. Once again, in order to have the right people on the team, it is important to include many others in the process to ensure leaving no stone unturned.

First, *compose a list of tasks* which must be performed by the team. By grouping this list according to those that are related, you will arrive at several team work categories based on what must be done.

GIFT DISCERNMENT

Finally, design a tool for finding out *what potential team members bring to the team*. Here you are looking for gifts, skills, talents, and areas of expertise. You can tell the strength and weakness, as well as the needs of the team, by evaluating this information periodically. Future vacant positions should also be filled only with team input.

Often churches make the mistake of equating good managers with good leaders. These are related, but separate, gifts. One is not superior to the other. However, it is unusual to find one person with both gifts. A healthy team concept does not demand that an organization find someone with both.

RECRUITMENT AND HIRING

When seeking to build a team, it is important to select future team members based on their training, gifts, skills, talents, and whatever else they bring to the business, ministry, or agency. In other words, it is critical that there is a solid match between the individual and the task.

While recruitment may be in the hands of one individual, the actual hiring of a team member should not be limited to just one individual. Large organizations usually have a department that is charged with the hiring procedure. In smaller operations, it is advisable to have two or three people involved.

Most larger operations have a written procedure that is called an orientation or *entrance procedure*. I recommend that even smaller operations put their procedures in writing.

The actual final decision to add to the team should involve the *employment application, several interviews, and background investigation*. Again, use several persons in the process.

As early as possible in the procedure, it is important to place an *information packet* in the hands of the prospect in order to guarantee that as many of his/her questions have been answered as possible prior to the initial interview. In addition to information about the organization, this packet should include a *tentative job description, information on salary and benefits, evaluation procedure, conflict resolution procedure, and "exit" procedure.*

It is becoming increasingly common for organizations to make use of a hiring tool called a *personality profile* to help match the individual with the task and with the other members of the team. Experts tell us that a person's personality style influences his or her leadership style. A caution to observe in the use of various employment tests: God helps us enhance our strengths and minimize our weaknesses. There is no way to test for this impact.

IDEAS THAT WORK IN TEAM-BUILDING

Finally, here are a number of suggestions that can lead to effective team-building:

1. Check the previous work record of the applicant by contacting past employers. Look for problems and negative trends.

2. A positive work environment is essential in building a unified team.

3. In order to know the needs of your team, it is important to ask and not assume.

4. Excellent timely communications will eliminate most problems.

5. Practice "catching people doing things right" and reward team members regularly.

6. Encourage creativity and problem-solving. Give credit where credit is due.

7. As often as possible, interview the prospect and his or her spouse. Doing so can be quite revealing.

8. Servant leaders must possess humility in abundance.

ADDITIONAL READING

Engstrom, Ted W., and Edward R. Dayton. *The Art of Management for Christian Leaders*. Grand Rapids, MI: Zondervan, 1987.

Peters, Tom. *Thriving on Chaos*. San Francisco: Harper & Row, 1988.

Rush, Myron. *Management: A Biblical Approach*. Wheaton, IL: Victor Books, 1985.

Van Fleet, James K. *The Twenty-two Biggest Mistakes Managers Make & How to Correct Them*. Englewood Cliffs, NJ: Prentice Hall, 1986.

Chapter 7

STRATEGIC PLANNING LEADERSHIP

Roland G. Hardy Jr.

In 1963, the United States sent its first military troops into Vietnam. A decision had been made to enter the war. As our troops began to occupy South Vietnamese villages, it became clear that the United States had forgotten something. The military leadership had failed to specify our mission. Was the mission to oversee a conflict between relatives, to serve as a peacekeeping agent, to provide non-combat military advice to the South Vietnamese, or what?

In addition to being saddled with an unclear mission, U.S. troops were ill-prepared for the fight. They knew very little about several critical items: Vietnamese culture and customs, the art of jungle warfare, and the enemy's military tactics. Confusion was the order of the day. The soldiers didn't know whether they were to function as military advisers or combat soldiers. The outcome was predictable. After twelve years of fighting, a sobering 50,000-plus fatalities, and untold injuries, the United States withdrew its troops without measurable success.

Why did the U.S. involvement end in defeat? Because the United States had forgotten the most basic element of warfare: a comprehensive strategic plan for winning.

WHY STRATEGIC PLANNING?

Unfortunately, this lack of focus is also common in Christian ministries. Church and ministry mission statements, when and if they exist, are generally so broad and vague that they fail to provide a clear definition of what the ministry is and what it should be doing. The organization finds itself unfocused and dabbling in everything from feeding the homeless to youth gang counseling. Its activities are dictated by what someone on the outside thinks it should be doing (the community, civic leaders, the government) rather than by its own mission statement. The result is that, at best, few key objectives are accomplished; and members and staff find themselves going around in circles until they just drop out.

To be effective in implementing its God-given vision, the church or ministry must begin by distilling its vision of its purpose into a concise mission statement. Although this is a difficult process at first, its value is priceless; and it gets easier each time the organization repeats the exercise.

WHAT IS STRATEGIC PLANNING?

Although definitions vary from planner to planner, there is some consensus among authors and managers regarding the essential elements involved in strategic planning: a purpose, objectives, external and internal assessments, a long-term strategy, realistic action plans, and regular evaluations. For the purpose of this chapter, I will define strategic planning as the process of:

- Identifying your purpose and objectives;

- Assessing the community around you as well as your internal strengths and weaknesses;

- Establishing realistic action plans; and

- Evaluating your performance in achieving your purpose and objectives.

WHO'S IN THE ROOM?

Strategic planning begins with determining who should be involved in the

Roland G. Hardy Jr.

planning process. In the African American church, planning participants tend to be limited to the pastor and the deacon, executive, or elder boards.

The problem with this approach is that it tends to be insular. That is, the planning process goes forward with a small group of people, keeping the church from the benefit of potentially insightful perspectives of lay ministers and others who may have their pulse on the congregation and/or the surrounding community. It limits the possibilities of creating a lasting, impactful vision for those whom the church will reach, and risks superficiality when important how-do-we-do-it detail is left out.

A better approach is to ensure involvement from the upper echelons of leadership (deacon, elders, trustees, steward/executive boards, senior and junior ministers), the lower echelons (ministry leaders, Sunday School teachers, lay readers), and what I like to call the "kitchen cabinet." This is that important group of members who, though they may not have an official ministry role, are active in the life of the church. These are the "church mothers," the people who are involved in prayer ministry, even those congregants who are vocal in their criticism and complaints. The point is that it is important to have the perspectives of a cross-section of congregants in order to have a plan that is robust and addresses the real needs of the members and of the surrounding community.

With many advisers they succeed.

~Proverbs 15:22

THE MISSION STATEMENT

Once the strategic planning team has been assembled, its initial task is to identify and document the organization's mission. This is accomplished in the form of a mission statement which defines the nature of the organization and its reason for existence. (See Examples 1 and 2.)

The mission statement establishes a common understanding of the extent and limits of the ministry and provides clear direction for its members, staff, and participants in the performance of their duties.

Notice in these examples that the mission statement is particular to the activity or organization. The church mission is broad; the "Year of the Family Ministry" mission statement is very specific. That's OK; the scope of the mission must be tailored to the size of the mission. Don't try to make a mission do more than it is supposed to do.

Example 1: Mt. Zion Baptist Church Mission Statement

Mt. Zion Baptist Church has been organized to:

- Promote the Gospel of Jesus Christ through public worship, personal and corporate evangelism, and missionary outreach.
- Teach and train its members in the observance of biblical Christianity.
- Conduct other activities designed to advance the kingdom of God through Jesus Christ.

Example 2: The Year of the Family Ministry Mission Statement

To mount a campaign designed to counteract the prevailing anti-Christian perspective of the family and to serve as a catalyst for the reintroduction of biblical family standards within the urban community.

OBJECTIVES

After completing the mission statement, the planning team is ready to establish objectives—the measurable accomplishments that lead to the fulfillment of the mission. These must be *specific, realistic/attainable*, and *measurable*. Those aren't just words. They mean something.

- *Specific*: The objective cannot be generic. "To be the best church in the city" is not a specific objective. What does that mean? If you don't see how you can get there, it's not specific enough.

- *Realistic/Attainable*: Don't try to hit impossible targets. There is nothing wrong with hitting difficult targets, but impossible is another thing altogether. If you're a $10,000 tithing church and you want to get to $1 million next year, you will probably be disappointed.

- *Measurable*: "To have more youth participation" is *not* measurable. "To increase youth attendance in our Sunday School by fifteen percent" is.

The setting of objectives is critical to the mission. You won't know you've achieved your objectives if you can't measure them. You'll be discouraged if you set them unattainably high or make them too vague or generic.

Example 3 illustrates a possible starter set of objectives for our hypothetical Mt. Zion Baptist Church. Example 4 represents the actual objectives for family ministry for a given year established by the planning team of the church.

Example 3: Mt. Zion Baptist Church Objectives

- Communicate the gospel message of Jesus Christ to every household in Greenville.
- Move church members to a state of spiritual maturity within a five-year period.
- Increase the number of male members by 250 within three years.
- Build a multipurpose facility to serve as a gym within ten years.

Take a close look at these objectives in Example 3. They are specific. They are realistic and attainable. Most importantly, they are measurable. See the numbers? "Every," "five-year period," "250" and "ten years." Anyone who looks at these objectives knows clearly what the goal is.

Example 4: The Year of the Family Ministry Objectives

- Develop a national prayer network to support urban families.
- Raise a positive, yet distinctly Christian, voice through the media, concerning the urban family.
- Mobilize and give greater exposure to Christian-based ministries committed to urban families.
- Promote and explore available resources to enhance urban families.
- Equip and empower the church in its ongoing ministry to families.
- Empower urban families.

These objectives in Example 4 are a bit more nebulous. They are specific, but short on measurability. What is it to "raise a positive ... voice?" What does it mean to "empower urban families?" These objectives could use some numbers, or some measure to help the team know when the goal has been hit.

EXTERNAL AND INTERNAL ASSESSMENTS

In order to determine the how-to's in accomplishing its objectives, the church or ministry must next assess what is going on around it as well as what is going on inside. While Mt. Zion Baptist Church can learn from strategies and tactics that have worked very well for other churches, the leadership team must keep in mind that what worked for another church may be totally inappropriate for Mt. Zion for a variety of reasons too numerous to mention here.

A large number of well-intentioned church projects have failed as a result of the local leadership not undertaking external and internal assessments with respect to their stated mission and objectives. The questions in Example 5 might be addressed profitably by Mt. Zion Baptist Church in order to properly assess the viability of its work as well as its strengths and weaknesses.

Example 5: External and Internal Assessment

- How many households are there, and what is the access to them?
- How many households are headed by single females?
- How many households include teenage mothers?
- What is the community's socioeconomic profile (average income per household, homeowners vs. renters, car owners, etc.)?
- Is the community receptive to receiving the gospel through a door-to-door campaign, media campaign, or outdoor evangelistic meetings?
- What is the church's image in the community?
- What is the age and gender composition of the church's membership?
- How many members attend church regularly?
- How many mature Christians attend the church?
- Does the church have trained personnel to accomplish its objectives?
- What is the church's financial position?
- What are the other churches or ministries in the area that service the same population?

Suppose the Mt. Zion Baptist Church scheduled an evangelistic door-to-door campaign for Greenville in the evenings for the first six weeks of summer. The church assembles an evangelistic team and begins training it. The team consists of four women and two men. They choose to use Bible tracts that show a White mother and father teaching their children the Scriptures around the kitchen table. The team shows up at the church at 6:30 p.m. on the first night of the campaign. They pair up and begin going to the homes in the city. After two weeks of the campaign, the team has been able to share their message with five people. Most of the homes refused to answer the door. Those who did answer said they were not interested. The five people who were cordial enough to listen to the presentation were distracted frequently by children.

Question: What objective was the campaign designed to meet? *Answer:* communication of the gospel of Jesus Christ to every household in Greenville.

An assessment of the campaign would lead us to the obvious conclusion that it was not successful in accomplishing the objective. Why? Greenville is a city of 100,000—seventy percent of whom are African American, twenty-eight percent Caucasian, and two percent Asian American. Forty percent of the 100,000 people are under the age of 25. Ninety percent of the households have income of less than $20,000 per year. Seventy percent of the families were started by teenage females. The crime rate is so high that the people don't answer their doors after dark. Most of the homes have chains or bars across the windows and doors. Further, there are three hundred Christian churches in Greenville, and twenty percent of the population attends church on a regular basis. Every summer at least one church conducts a door-to-door evangelistic campaign handing out Bible tracts. The church has a reputation of being irrelevant, outdated, and hypocritical.

The door-to-door campaign did not accomplish the church's objective because the church did not consider what was going on in the community in its planning. Had it done so, it would have concluded that a door-to-door campaign would be ineffective, that its evangelistic team was too small, and that its materials did not relate to most of the people.

The planning team should have chosen a plan of action that recognized the impact of crime on the access to community homes, understood the skepticism of the community toward the church, incorporated a gospel presentation relevant to the large percentage of unwed, teenage mothers and youth, and facilitated partnering among the various churches and ministries to maximize resources. If this planning approach had been taken, the likelihood of Mt. Zion's accomplishing its objective would have been much greater.

ACTION PLAN

> ### Example 6: Mt. Zion Baptist Church Action Plan
>
> **Objective:** To move church members to a state of spiritual maturity within five years.
> **Goal:** To assess the spiritual maturity level of all members by (specify date).
>
> **Action Point 1:** Establish standards for measuring spiritual maturity by (specify date).
> **Responsible person:** Pastor
>
> **Action Point 2:** Establish evaluation process by (specify date).
> **Responsible persons:** Pastor and board
>
> **Action Point 3:** Prepare necessary tools for evaluation by (specify date).
> **Responsible person:** Delegated by pastor
>
> **Action Point 4:** Conduct evaluation of members by (specify date).
> **Responsible persons:** Pastor and board
>
> **Objective:** To move church members to a state of spiritual maturity within five years.
> **Goal:** To begin spiritual growth process by (specify date).
>
> **Action Point 1:** Establishment of spiritual growth process by pastor and deacon board by (specify date).
>
> **Action Point 2:** Training of leaders by pastor by (specify date).
>
> **Action Point 3:** Completion of initial leadership training by (specify date).
>
> **Action Point 4:** Assignment of families to leaders by (specify date).

The strategy will dictate what the organization's action plan will look like. The *action plan* takes each objective and gives it a life cycle from beginning point to achievement. This life cycle is commonly expressed in terms of goals, action points, and timetables.

For each objective, there should be a set of goals, action points, and a timetable. Each action point has a series of steps with corresponding timetables which serve as building blocks toward the accomplishment of the objectives. Accomplishing the objectives leads to the achievement of the organization's mission.

Note: The terms "goals" and "objectives" are sometimes used interchangeably. Some organizations use the word "goals" where we use the term "objectives." As long as the church/organization is clear on the definition of the terms, these different uses are perfectly alright.

Notice in Example 6 in the goals and points that we ask for a specific date for accomplishing actions. These dates are extremely important. Without a date specified, the action point gets pushed back, as other priorities take precedence. There is something about a deadline that moves people to act.

EVALUATION

The last phase of strategic planning involves an evaluation to determine if the objectives have been met. Evaluation should be built into the process from the outset and conducted at predetermined intervals, such as quarterly or semiannually. During this phase, the organization performs an assessment of its personnel, resources, objectives, and strategies. The evaluation must include appropriate rewards for accomplishments, encouragement, and—where necessary—adjustments.

A great way is to create a grid that details each of your objectives, goals, and action points, and allows space to indicate whether each of these was met and when. You may have set a February 1 date to, for example, complete initial leadership training, when the actual completion date was March 1. So the action point was met; it was just a little later. Those details are good to know; they set the basis for more realistic timetables for the next cycle of ministry.

CONCLUSION

The goal of maximum stewardship demands that churches and ministries properly plan the most effective use of their opportunities and resources. Satan continues to roam the streets of our communities seeking those whom he may devour. The war is on for our culture. If you don't *plan* to win, don't get in the war.

Chapter 8

FAMILY SUCCESSION: PASSING LEADERSHIP ON TO YOUR CHILDREN

Diane Proctor Reeder

Every chapter in this book has addressed leadership from an institutional perspective. I'd like to go another way.

"Are you a teacher?"

I can't tell you how many times I have been asked that question. Both my parents were in education, and both of them thought education would be a great profession for me.

"You are such a teacher."

I get that every time I present to a group. I am emphatically *not* a teacher. I am a writer; I speak to groups about what I write, and I am asked to lead Bible studies and Sunday-school classes at my own church and at conferences. And so I tell people what I am.

"I am a writer and a playwright," I tell them.

"I edit and package books for people," I might say to someone else. "I do event planning and public relations," might be my message for yet another group.

But I never say, "I am a teacher."

Nevertheless, people *still* say what a good "teacher" I am. One day, walking out of church, a man stopped me enthusiastically. He mistook me for one of his high-school teachers.

No matter how hard I try, I can't seem to get away from the "teacher" moniker. I guess it's in my genes.

Spiritual genes, that is.

Our connection to our parents and our ancestry does not dictate that we should automatically do what they do. But it does inform the work that God has ordained for us. In other words, we inherit more than just their DNA. We "inherit" the values and principles that they hand down to us. And sometimes, we inherit—and advance—the work that they do.

Even as I write this, I am writing very carefully, saying something very specific and wanting to make the fine distinctions that need to be made between passing down a *profession* and passing down a *life*. After all, there are parents who want their children to do exactly what they've done. Pastors sometimes try to pass on the pastorate to their children. Corporate heads try to make their sons or daughters (usually sons) the "heir apparent." Heads of state sometimes do the same thing (e.g., George H. W. Bush to George W. Bush). Sometimes those transitions are God-ordained, and sometimes they are not. It is not our place to be the final arbiter of those transitions. God has the final answer there.

It's just that, too often, parents try to shoehorn or pigeonhole their children into doing what they do. That is one of the best ways I know to blunt God's direction. Imagine this conversation between the Hebrew patriarch Abraham and his father, Terah. Remember that Terah's chosen profession was idolmaker. He crafted the images that those in the city of Ur, where they lived, used in their idol-worshipping ceremonies. Terah had not yet heard of the God who ultimately spoke to his son.

Terah: Abram
Abram: Yes, father?
Terah: What are your plans for the future, son?
Abram: I don't know.
Terah: Let me teach you the craft of idol-making. It is a good profession and pays me very well.
Abram: I don't know.
Terah: You are going to have to raise your family. You need something solid to depend on.

The Bible does not say that Abram and his father had that conversation. We only know that God called Abram after his father died, after Terah actually took his son Abram, daughter-in-law Sarai, and nephew Lot and left the idol-worshipping city of Ur. He intended to go to Canaan, but he stopped instead in the city of Haran.

We can pull a lot of riches out of this short narrative. God called Abram to do something his father had not done. He called Abram into a special relationship, even a friendship, with himself. The benefits of that special relationship redound to us today. That special relationship, and Abram's obedient response, have impacted the lives of literally billions of people, including all of us who call ourselves "Christian."

God called Abram to the "original intent" of his father. Terah, remember, was headed for Canaan, the promised land that God would eventually carve out for the now-named Abraham and the Hebrew people.

> *Terah took his son Abram, his grandson Lot son of Haran, and his daughter-in-law Sarai, the wife of his son Abram, and together they set out from Ur of the Chaldeans to go to Canaan. But when they came to Haran, they settled there.*
>
> ~Genesis 11:31

But God did not call Abram to the "original profession" of his father. Terah made idols. Abram, who became Abraham, was certainly not destined for that.

> *No longer will you be called Abram; your name will be Abraham, for I have made you a father of many nations.*
>
> ~Genesis 17:5

Abraham, as he was now called, was destined to populate nations with his genes, but also with his spiritual heritage. We are the beneficiaries of that heritage today.

You probably, if you think about it, have your own personal spiritual heritage story. I certainly do, both as one who is the beneficiary of a heritage, and one who has, with my late husband, despite our own faults and failures, passed that down to our children as well.

First, the beneficiary side. In 2000, I self-published a book. The name was *A Diary of Joseph: A Spiritual Journey Through Time.* It is a book that imagines the journey of the biblical Joseph (the Old Testament Joseph, son of

Jacob) in poetry and prose. It includes imaginary conversations between God and Joseph as he goes through the permutations of favored son, hated brother, trusted servant, falsely accused, imprisoned, and then viceroy of Egypt. The conversations parallel my own family's ups and downs, when my husband of twelve years was diagnosed with acute leukemia, then experienced his (and our) own sets of highs and lows as he went through chemotherapy, a harrowing bone marrow transplant, and more than two years of relative health before going home to be with the Lord in 1998. The book's genesis was in 1987, and the idea hung on stubbornly until 1994 when Terry was diagnosed. It was a whirlwind of suffering, and reprieve, that went into the writing of this, my first book.

But the real genesis was decades before. Shortly after my dad's death in 2000, I found out from my mother that *her* father always told her the Joseph story, and that she loved to hear it. Then she showed me a small black note-book. It was a looseleaf binder from my grandmother, and it detailed poetry and a year-by-year listing of every book she read during the 30s and '40s. I was blown away. To think that my grandfather talked about this Joseph I was now writing about, and that my grandmother was such an avid reader—a trait, in fact, that she passed on to my mother, who passed it on to me.

Here's the clincher: Both my parents were longtime public school edu-cators. I felt rich with legacy.

So what happened with my children? As a writer, I passed down that skill and so their best grades were in English. My son wrote sparking prose and book reviews in high school, and wrote a knockout college essay about his late father. When she got to college, my daughter was, in her freshman year, selected as one of the editors (my profession) of the school science journal.

Now, her chosen profession is animal cancer research—about as far from writing and editing as you can get. But she has a skill—writing—that she will have for life.

My son David took a different direction. Now, before he passed, his dad started a cleaning business. Terry used to take David with him to clean our church, which was he and his partner Anthony's first major contract. "You're going to own this one day, Terry would tell David, showing him how to do the sinks in the bathroom and the floors. David, age six, was so very proud to be going with his dad. The name of the business was Cleanco. "Are we doing Cleanco, Dad?" he would ask, eyes shining with excitement.

Fast-forward eighteen years. It's hard to believe that the time has passed so quickly. David comes home one day and announces to me that he's going to start a cleaning business. He's found a franchise that parcels out office cleaning contracts for a fee, and he's decided to save his money and buy one.

"I could do it as an employee of the company, but I want to do it under my own business name," he explains to me proudly.

"What are you going to name it?" I ask.

He says, with the gleam in his eye I had seen years before: "Cleanco. Just like Dad."

I am excited for him. I am excited for both my children, who are emerging from the other side of two very painful, too-early deaths—their father and their grandfather, my dad—with grace and determination. The same determination my Dad had when he decided he would rather continue his direct involvement with young people as a teacher than "going downtown," as he put it, as an educational supervisor. The same determination my Mom had when she, with a small toddler (me) worked, went to school at night, and never failed to read me my bedtime story and put me to sleep. The determination of their other grandparents, Jessie and Ray Reeder, who literally dug the basement of their newly built house in Ohio, and who worked hard as a teacher and Ford worker, respectively, to provide for their two children and put them through college.

I could tell you more. I could tell you of a camp that my children's grandfather helped to build, and their grandmother helped to run. Circle Y Ranch in Bangor, Michigan—a Christian camp that ministers to kids in Detroit and Chicago, a place that I, my husband, and both my children have thought of as home. We have a rich heritage, one that nothing and no one can take away.

Do you have a spiritual lineage? Rejoice! You have favor from God because of your parents, grandparents, and/or great-grandparents. As we talk about succession of leadership, there is no more important succession than the one that passes down from grandparent to parent to child.

Know therefore that the LORD your God is God; he is the faithful God, keeping his covenant of love to a thousand generations of those who love him and keep his commandments.

~Deuteronomy 7:9

For more information, visit www.ADiaryofJoseph.com.

Chapter 9

SEVEN ESSENTIAL QUESTIONS FOR LEADERSHIP SUCCESSION

Diane Proctor Reeder

B y now, you are probably all too familiar with the story: Dynamic African American pastor regales the congregation every week with his (or her) Biblical exegesis. The church is full of substantive, holistic programs and members are being added every month. It is *the* place to be. "Did you hear Pastor last week? He really tore it up." is heard often among members, who tell their friends, saved and unsaved: "You have to come to my church and hear the service."

Unfortunately, there are cracks in the story. Despite a full complement of ministers, the pastor speaks virtually every week, save the occasional out-of-town trip. He (and usually it is a "he"; women have just recently come to the fore in terms of pastoral leadership in the African American Church) is virtually everywhere, preaching and teaching and visiting the sick... until, one day, he takes ill or tragically, dies. For thirty to fifty years, the congregation has grown accustomed to his face... and his preaching style... and his leadership.

You know what happens next. The church elders or leadership starts the great search for a pastor. There is confusion and bitter debate as candidates, both inside and outside the church, are selected for interview and consideration. Finally, a new pastor is chosen... and half the church leaves. The other half is just waiting to see what will happen. Invariably, the new pastor never measures up; how could he or she possibly do so? The members have made the former pastor larger than life, with bigger shoes to fill than any human being could possibly be expected to do. For years, the church limps along; donations dwindle, and the church is merely a shadow of its former self. And the promise of God to enlarge the church's territory and increase her borders remains an unfulfilled dream. It's a frequently occurring story that makes you want to cry.

But it doesn't have to happen. Here, for your consideration as leaders, are seven key questions to ask yourself. Consider them to be "examination" questions—not to see whether you are "in the faith," because you already are, but instead to see whether you are following God's principles to ensure that leadership transitions from one generation to the next in an orderly fashion that elicits excitement and buy-in from the congregation, instead of despair and confusion.

QUESTION #1: HAVE I LEARNED THE DELEGATION LESSON?

The next day Moses took his seat to serve as judge for the people, and they stood around him from morning till evening. When his father-in-law saw all that Moses was doing for the people, he said, "What is this you are doing for the people? Why do you alone sit as judge, while all these people stand around you from morning till evening?"

Moses answered him, "Because the people come to me to seek God's will. Whenever they have a dispute, it is brought to me, and I decide between the parties and inform them of God's decrees and instructions."

Moses' father-in-law replied, "What you are doing is not good. You and these people who come to you will only wear yourselves out. The work is too heavy for you; you cannot handle it alone. Listen now to me and I will give you some advice, and may God be with you. You must be the people's representative before God and bring their disputes to him. Teach them his decrees and instructions, and show them the way they are to live and how they are to behave. But select capable men from all the people—men who fear God, trustworthy men who hate dishonest gain—and appoint them as officials over thousands, hundreds, fifties and tens. Have them serve as judges for the people at all times, but have them bring every difficult case to you; the simple cases they can decide themselves. That will make your load lighter, because they will share it

*with you. If you do this and God so commands, you will be able to stand
the strain, and all these people will go home satisfied."*

Moses listened to his father-in-law and did everything he said.
~Exodus 18:13–24

Moses was at his wits' end. He was exhausted and could probably barely
manage to crawl back to his sleeping quarters for a few short hours before
he was once again bombarded by questions large and small from the hundreds of thousands of Hebrews he had led so aptly to freedom. Empowered
by God, he had seen miracle after miracle. He probably saw himself as
a kind of Superman. In fact, we know he did, because one day he made an
independent-of-God decision to hit a rock and make it produce water, when God
had only told him to speak to the rock. And of course, Superman never gets tired.

But Moses was bone-weary, and sleep deprivation does strange things to
the mind. We will never know what answers he gave during those fog-filled
times when his body longed to recline and his eyes yearned to close. Yet he
kept heroically on, until one day....

His father-in-law Jethro, himself a priest, confronted Moses. "You can't
keep this up." he said. "You're going to collapse under the weight of these
people." Then, Jethro gave him perhaps the first-ever organizational development plan in human history.

It worked! No one was happier than Moses. The Bible is silent on some
of the details, but we can almost be sure that there were some complainers
in the bunch. Can't you just hear some of the Israelites saying, "Who are
you? I want to talk to Moses. What, I'm not good enough to talk to him now?"
After all, we're doing the same thing today. "No, I don't want to talk with the
associate minister; I want to talk to Pastor."

Moses was so consumed with his responsibility to lead that he literally
didn't give himself time to think about what he was doing. He had been given
a heady task by God, and given our all-too-human nature, that undoubtedly
reflected itself in how he approached his work. Maybe he became a bit of a
"control freak." It would be understandable; after all, he spoke directly to
God, even got to peek at him from the back. It was a heady experience, and
probably made him think that he *had* to keep control in order to ensure the
safe passage of his people from Egypt to the land of promise. It took a wise,
older man to look at the organizational reality and see another way to govern.

As a pastor or ministry leader, do you have the sober wisdom and godly faith it takes to delegate? Do you feel the need to control, or can you entrust your leader-mentee to do what they have learned from you? Examine yourself, and see how you would grade yourself on the Delegation Question.

QUESTION #2: DO I HAVE A YOUNGER PERSON THAT I HAVE ENGAGED IN LIFELONG MENTORING?

Once again, we consider Moses. Once Jethro lovingly challenged him on the delegation question, he was able to carefully choose, well ahead of his last days of leadership, a faithful young person to succeed him as the leader. That person, as we all know, was Joshua. Joshua, the eyewitness to a full demonstration of God's power in ministry, in prayer, in building community, in investigation.

Joshua had seen power and authority conferred on Moses by God Himself. Even before that, he had watched Moses bravely, at risk of death, confront Pharaoh, and his own feet walked the floor of the parted Red Sea.

He had seen the power of prayer. Most importantly, he had seen the prayer of a sincere leader who was simply pouring out his heart to God in complaint. "What am I to do with these people?" Moses pleaded. "They're about ready to stone me!" No flowery language, no thees and thous, just a frustrated man sharing his frustration with the only One who could provide the answer. For Joshua, that certainly had to be a powerful moment.

Joshua saw his leader interact one-on-one with God himself. But his leader, Moses, also exercised wisdom. He knew that Joshua would be his successor, and so he brought him into his most intimate inner circle with God.

The LORD said to Moses, "Come up to me on the mountain and stay here, and I will give you the tablets of stone with the law and commandments I have written for their instruction."

Then Moses set out with Joshua his aide, and Moses went up on the mountain of God. He said to the elders, "Wait here for us until we come back to you. Aaron and Hur are with you, and anyone involved in a dispute can go to them."

~Exodus 24:12–14

Moses had by now learned the art of delegation quite well. He trusted Aaron and Hur to handle things in his absence, but significantly he took the very one he expected to lead after him: Joshua. That was valuable preparation for Moses's mentee. Joshua soaked it in, and found himself prepared for the leadership moment when it finally came. Moses was preparing Joshua for his destiny.

The LORD would speak to Moses face to face, as one speaks to a friend. Then Moses would return to the camp, but his young aide Joshua son of Nun did not leave the tent.

~Exodus 33:11

He asked the LORD, "Why have you brought this trouble on your servant? What have I done to displease you that you put the burden of all these people on me?"

~Numbers 11:11

Joshua was in the tabernacle with Moses when he spoke to God "face to face." He was with Moses in his most intimate moments with God. Significantly, he saw Moses argue and wrestle with God on behalf of his people. And he saw Moses complain to God about the burden of leadership. Your "lifelong" mentee should similarly see you up-close and personal. You should be open to them seeing your highest highs and your lowest lows.

When the time came for Joshua's faith to be tested, he passed with flying colors.

Joshua son of Nun and Caleb son of Jephunneh, who were among those who had explored the land, tore their clothes and said to the entire Israelite assembly, "The land we passed through and explored is exceedingly good. If the LORD is pleased with us, he will lead us into that land, a land flowing with milk and honey, and will give it to us."

~Numbers 14:6–8

Certainly the time he spent with Moses, seeing his intimate interaction with God, and his deep faith and commitment to obedience, made a significant impression on young Joshua. Finally, God determined when it was time for Moses to commission his charge:

*So the L*ORD *said to Moses, "Take Joshua son of Nun, a man in whom is the spirit of leadership, and lay your hand on him. Have him stand before Eleazar the priest and the entire assembly and commission him in their presence. Give him some of your authority so the whole Israelite community will obey him. He is to stand before Eleazar the priest, who will obtain decisions for him by inquiring of the Urim before the L*ORD*. At his command he and the entire community of the Israelites will go out, and at his command they will come in." Moses did as the L*ORD *commanded him. He took Joshua and had him stand before Eleazar the priest and the whole assembly. Then he laid his hands on him and commissioned him, as the L*ORD *instructed through Moses.*

~Numbers 27:18–23

Notice that God was the one who told Moses who should succeed him in leadership. Be careful choosing the one in whom you make a lifelong investment. Make sure that God has spoken before you act.

QUESTION #3: AM I MENTORING MY FAMILY? HOW DOES MY EXAMPLE LOOK TO THEM? WHAT AM I PASSING ON TO THEM?

The father-son relationship between David and Solomon provides the best examples of 1) what to do and 2) what NOT to do in a mentoring relationship. As a leader of God's people who committed adultery and tried to cover it up; and as a father who failed to discipline his sons with tragic, fratricidal results, David was not exactly a model of moral behavior.

But when it really counted, David stepped up to the task. He prepared the way for his son to be a great king, by unselfishly, and under the direction of God Himself, passed on the vision to build the Temple of God. David actually had the desire to build the Temple, but God had other plans.

*Go and tell David my servant, Thus saith the L*ORD*, Thou shalt not build me an house to dwell in: For I have not dwelt in an house since the day that I brought up Israel unto this day; but have gone from tent to tent, and from one tabernacle to another.*

~1 Chronicles 17:4–5 KJV

Diane Proctor Reeder

And so David, in one of his last acts of obedience, set up his son Solomon for success.

Then King David said to the whole assembly: "My son Solomon, the one whom God has chosen, is young and inexperienced. The task is great, because this palatial structure is not for man but for the LORD God. With all my resources I have provided for the temple of my God—gold for the gold work, silver for the silver, bronze for the bronze, iron for the iron and wood for the wood, as well as onyx for the settings, turquoise, stones of various colors, and all kinds of fine stone and marble—all of these in large quantities. Besides, in my devotion to the temple of my God I now give my personal treasures of gold and silver for the temple of my God, over and above everything I have provided for this holy temple: three thousand talents of gold (gold of Ophir) and seven thousand talents of refined silver, for the overlaying of the walls of the buildings, for the gold work and the silver work, and for all the work to be done by the craftsmen. Now, who is willing to consecrate themselves to the LORD today?"

Then the leaders of families, the officers of the tribes of Israel, the commanders of thousands and commanders of hundreds, and the officials in charge of the king's work gave willingly.

~1 Chronicles 29:1–6

Are you preparing your children to build beyond your capacity or gifting? Reflect on the example of David.

QUESTION #4: AM I PASSING ON A HERITAGE OF SPIRITUAL POWER?

So Elijah went from there and found Elisha son of Shaphat. He was plowing with twelve yoke of oxen, and he himself was driving the twelfth pair. Elijah went up to him and threw his cloak around him.

~1 Kings 19:19

Thus began a close mentoring relationship between the prophet Elijah and his protégé Elisha. The latter traveled with the former as he raised the dead to life, confronted kings, and battled with false prophets. That cloak, or "mantle," of Elijah's would be significant a bit later in his and Elisha's mentoring relationship. When Elijah was nearing death, and God "took" him to his celestial home in a chariot, Elisha used his cloak, as did his mentor earlier, to part the waters of the Jordan River.

There is a spiritual power in mentoring that must be reckoned with. As you are in close proximity to your protégé, some of the power that God has given you will sometimes be imparted to them. Consider whether you are truly walking in God's power as you think about your mentoring relationships. And consider this: Elisha actually performed *more* miracles than his mentor. If you are walking in God's power, those who come after you are destined to do greater things.

Very truly I tell you, whoever believes in me will do the works I have been doing, and they will do even **greater things** *than these, because I am going to the Father.*

~John 14:12

QUESTION #5: AM I LOYAL TO MY MENTEE(S) REGARDLESS OF PUBLIC OPINION?

The role of Barnabas in the ministry of Paul is an overlooked story: *When he came to Jerusalem, he tried to join the disciples, but they were all afraid of him, not believing that he really was a disciple. But Barnabas took him and brought him to the apostles. He told them how Saul on his journey had seen the Lord and that the Lord had spoken to him, and how in Damascus he had preached fearlessly in the name of Jesus.*

~Acts 9:26–27

Remember: Paul was an enemy of the church who had the original "Damascus Road" experience. It was perfectly understandable that the other Christians would look askance at him. Was he sincere? Was he trying to sabotage from the "inside?" Who was this new Paul?

Barnabas listened to the Lord. Fearlessly—and this certainly took courage—he convinced his fellow believers that Paul's conversion was the real thing.

Do you have the courage to back a mentee when others are skeptical? Do you listen to God...or to your fellow church members when recommending someone for ministry or leadership? If God can change a Saul to a Paul, what is possible with those whom you might be discipling?

QUESTION #6: DO I HAVE AN "INNER CIRCLE" OF MENTEES, WITH WHOM I SPEND PRIME TIME IN TRAINING?

Jesus had a community of people that he taught. He had the twelve disciples with whom he spent concentrated time... and then he had the three disciples into whom he poured his life. Those three were Peter, James, and John. Peter authored two of the epistles; James authored one; and John authored one gospel, three epistles, and Revelation.

As a leader, you should similarly work on three levels. If you are a pastor, you have your congregation, your leadership team, and your inner circle of individuals with whom you work. Like Jesus, you should be spending most of your time with those few people, and letting them—and the congregation—explicitly know that the "baton" will be passed to them at some future, God-directed point. They are your "Peter, James, and John" (though there might be a Mary or a Patrice there as well).

Your next group is the leadership team. These are your "twelve disciples." The group may be smaller or larger, but again, you're spending a good amount of time teaching and pouring into them.

The final group is your entire congregation and your church's neighborhood. Those are, so to speak, the "multitudes." With these individuals, you will speak, and preach, but your inner circle and your disciples will do a lot of the heavy lifting, mentoring, and intense teaching that this group requires.

QUESTION #7: AM I PROMOTING CROSS-CULTURAL EXCHANGE?

It is said that Sunday morning is the most segregated hour of the week. The New Testament Church was not that way. The New Testament Church was composed of Jews, Greeks, Romans, former Stoic philosophers, former idol worshipers, Africans, Syrians, Jewish Zealots whose original goal was to overthrow the Roman kingdom, and many others. Take a look:

Chapter 9

When the day of Pentecost came, they were all together in one place. Suddenly a sound like the blowing of a violent wind came from heaven and filled the whole house where they were sitting. They saw what seemed to be tongues of fire that separated and came to rest on each of them. All of them were filled with the Holy Spirit and began to speak in other tongues as the Spirit enabled them.

Now there were staying in Jerusalem God-fearing Jews from every nation under heaven. When they heard this sound, a crowd came together in bewilderment, because each one heard their own language being spoken. Utterly amazed, they asked: "Aren't all these who are speaking Galileans? Then how is it that each of us hears them in our native language? **Parthians, Medes and Elamites; residents of Mesopotamia, Judea and Cappadocia, Pontus and Asia, Phrygia and Pamphylia, Egypt and the parts of Libya near Cyrene; visitors from Rome (both Jews and converts to Judaism); Cretans and Arabs**—*we hear them declaring the wonders of God in our own tongues!"*

~Acts 2:1–11 *(emphasis added)*

Isn't it significant that on the very day that God established his new church, he made sure that the widest possible range of ethnicities was represented? I would suggest to you that this was part of the early church's power. Certainly the New Testament church was far from perfect, but they definitely got the message that God's love was for all people, and that the physical and genetic and geographical distinctions were made inconsequential in the blinding light of God's love and acceptance.

So in Christ Jesus you are all children of God through faith, for all of you who were baptized into Christ have clothed yourselves with Christ. There is neither Jew nor Gentile, neither slave nor free, nor is there male and female, for you are all one in Christ Jesus.

~Galatians 3:26–28

The Christian Church today can take a lesson from these powerful stories in the book of Acts. Here is a particularly relevant lesson in evangelism from the apostle Paul:

Diane Proctor Reeder

While Paul was waiting for them in Athens, he was greatly distressed to see that the city was full of idols. So he reasoned in the synagogue with both Jews and God-fearing Greeks, as well as in the market-place day by day with those who happened to be there. A group of Epicurean and Stoic philosophers began to debate with him. Some of them asked, "What is this babbler trying to say?" Others remarked, "He seems to be advocating foreign gods." They said this because Paul was preaching the good news about Jesus and the resurrection. Then they took him and brought him to a meeting of the Areopagus, where they said to him, "May we know what this new teaching is that you are presenting? You are bringing some strange ideas to our ears, and we would like to know what they mean." (All the Athenians and the foreigners who lived there spent their time doing nothing but talking about and listening to the latest ideas.)

Paul then stood up in the meeting of the Areopagus and said: "People of Athens! I see that in every way you are very religious. For as I walked around and looked carefully at your objects of worship, I even found an altar with this inscription: TO AN UNKNOWN GOD. So you are ignorant of the very thing you worship—and this is what I am going to proclaim to you.

"The God who made the world and everything in it is the Lord of heaven and earth and does not live in temples built by human hands. And he is not served by human hands, as if he needed anything. Rather, he himself gives everyone life and breath and everything else. From one man he made all the nations, that they should inhabit the whole earth; and he marked out their appointed times in history and the boundaries of their lands. God did this so that they would seek him and perhaps reach out for him and find him, though he is not far from any one of us. 'For in him we live and move and have our being.' As some of your own poets have said, 'We are his offspring.'

"Therefore since we are God's offspring, we should not think that the divine being is like gold or silver or stone—an image made by human design and skill. In the past God overlooked such ignorance, but now he commands all people everywhere to repent. For he has set a day

when he will judge the world with justice by the man he has ap-
pointed. He has given proof of this to everyone by raising him from
the dead."

When they heard about the resurrection of the dead, some of them
sneered, but others said, "We want to hear you again on this subject."
At that, Paul left the Council. **Some of the people became fol-**
lowers of Paul and believed.

~Acts 17:16–34 *(emphasis added)*

So we see Paul evangelizing a group of people very much unlike him.
He was Jewish and they were Greek. They had a completely different per-
ception of God.

Did Paul come and berate them? Did he lord his religion over them? No!
He met them where they were in their belief. He acknowledged and respected
the fact that they were religious. He quoted their philosophers. Then, he piv-
oted to the saving message of Jesus Christ. It is probably one of the most bril-
liant examples of cross-cultural evangelism that we could emulate.

The church will grow as its various members begin to see the power of
diversity in building God's kingdom.

And so, as we look at the various examples and methods for leadership
succession, as we look at ways to confer "Elijah's mantle" to the next generation, let us consider these examples from the Scriptures, and take note.

I BEQUEATH

Last Will and Testament

FROM: Summit Members

TO: The Next Generation

Being of sound mind, the members of The Summit pass on to you, not methods, but principles. Not control, but a relinquishing of control to the Holy Spirit that resides within you. Take these riches and employ them to God's fit use.

- A love for God and his Word.

- A mindset of living transformationally.

- A strategy for reaching entire nations with the gospel.

- Accountability partners to help you maintain your integrity.

- A servant spirit.

- A focus on kingdom business.

- A love for the unchurched.

- Unity of the Spirit.

- Five generations of leadership—from Mary McLeod Bethune to Martin Luther King Jr. to Tom Skinner to Matt Parker to YOU ... and a firm foundation from which you can soar.

- Our love!